Inspiring WOMEN

HOW REAL WOMEN SUCCEED IN BUSINESS

Michelle Rosenberg

crimson

This edition first published in Great Britain 2007 by
Crimson Publishing, a division of Crimson Business Ltd
Westminster House
Kew Road
Richmond
Surrey
TW9 2ND

A catalogue record for this book is available from the British library.

ISBN 978 1 85458 410 6

Printed and bound by Mega Printing, Turkey

Contents

Acknowledgements

I would like to thank:

All the women featured in *Inspiring Women* for the time and effort given so generously and graciously.

Holly, Ian and David at Crimson, for enabling me to fulfil a long-held ambition; Lianne and Beth for their enthusiasm and fantastic support.

My family – Mum, Dad and my brother Jamie for always being there, and my friend Mel for supporting the idea from the very beginning.

My husband and best friend, Jeremy; for always telling me I could do it, for not putting up a fight for my time once he realised he'd have sole possession of the remote control and for giving me our beautiful daughters.

Michelle Rosenberg
July 2007

For my daughters, Lola and Madison
and for Grandma

Introduction

Always fascinated by the role of women in history, in society, in the home and in the workplace, I wanted to focus particularly on those entrepreneurs who put their money where their mouth is and actually fulfil their ambitions rather than just talk about them. I wanted to illustrate that there is no 'one size fits all' model in today's female society. Each of the women profiled here is different in her own way, and their individual journeys reflect that.

Perhaps both my interest in writing and yours in reading about these 'inspiring women' is reflective of our mutual need for reassurance that entrepreneurial and business success is achievable – whether through setting up on our own or taking on the mantle of another brand. Most of the women featured here founded their own companies, although I wanted also to include a few others, such as Penny Newman of Cafédirect, who were brought into a business at a later stage because of their expertise in a particular sector. Their dedication and determination are just as indefatigable and their achievements equally inspiring. Without them, their 'inherited' businesses may not be where they are today.

Just as I knew what I wanted this book to be, I was adamant what I wanted it not to be. I wasn't interested in perpetuating the ridiculous myth of the 'superwoman'; I don't believe it is possible for a woman to be all things to all people in equal measure. Instead, I wanted to show that women achievers can be 'normal', generally down to earth, friendly and approachable, and that, like everyone else, they struggle to balance the various responsibilities in their lives. I think in the past we have done ourselves a huge disservice by putting women achievers on pedestals whose dizzying heights we have not a chance of reaching.

Many of the women I spoke with for this book are mothers. Not all, but a large proportion. Indeed, perhaps the reason we see so many mothers starting their own businesses is a reflection of their frustration with a corporate world which continues to fail them so miserably. For them, something always has to give. One entrepreneur put a fine finger on it when she said that in trying to be the perfect mother, wife and businesswoman, she was only succeeding in failing miserably at all of them.

I wanted to portray the variety of ways in which these women manage. Some decided to seek out full-time childcare to enable them to get on with their day-to-day 'office' job, while others made a firm decision to work only three or four days a week in order to spend time with the family. A number of women still deliberately chose to grow the business slowly in order to retain some semblance of work/life balance for themselves and their staff. Those women without children also had work/life considerations and often had to rely heavily on the support of their partners to allow them to achieve their goals.

It is a cliché and yet a truism that women are better multi-taskers than men. Frankly, we have to be! We are the wives, mothers, daughters and partners as well as the executives and entrepreneurs. Let's face it; whilst we've made great strides in what we can and have achieved, the bottom line is that if we do decide to pursue a career – whether full or part time – society still assumes we'll also be the primary carers for the family.

I wanted to illustrate that women can do things their way without feeling they have to behave as a man in order to make it. Indeed, the majority of the women who were interviewed believe it is their very gender which enables them to be so successful in harnessing the interest of their consumers.

Women are able, in a way most men probably can't, to use their emotion and intuition to promote a business concept that is part commerce and part social philanthropy. In short, it seems the characteristics that were once perceived as weak are the very ones that enable today's businesswomen to be so attuned to the public zeitgeist! In many cases, it is precisely by being the so-called 'weaker' and 'fairer' sex that they are able to bring their own unique and successful approach to their business. Several of the companies profiled here reflect the social, environmental and ethical concerns shared by both founder and client.

From chocolates to clothing to coffee, consumers are increasingly aware of how and where their products are sourced. They are looking to forward-thinking businesses to set an example, and this is where being a woman in business can be such a powerful force for positive change – as well as for economic success. Of course, some may argue that these women shouldn't be defined by their gender; that they are simply business executives or entrepreneurs, and their sex has nothing to do with it, but I beg to differ. I believe that gender has everything to do with it.

Some of the women interviewed here have been on the receiving end of sexism in business, making them both furious and amused. Others have been praised by their staff for their determination not to try to be a man in order to succeed as a woman: none of the women make apologies for being feminine.

What links the women in this book is their passionate desire to do better, either to improve on a current service or product or to develop a new, innovative one. Each woman has a keen sense of social and moral responsibility which is reflected in their approaches to staff, suppliers and customers alike. That's not to doubt for one second their business expertise and brilliance. People mustn't mistake emotion and keen intuition as weaknesses, for these women aren't fools, and they don't suffer fools gladly. At the end of the day, they are all businesswomen, with their eyes on the bottom line. What makes them different, however, is that the bottom line isn't the only thing they care about. They are trying to turn perceived wisdoms on their head; to convince large retail groups heads that reputation and profits could be even better if they took a wider view on the implications of their actions and considered what would truly work for the consumer.

I wanted to demonstrate that you don't have to be a ruthless, chained-to-your-desk ball-breaker to 'make it'. In fact, I would argue that these women are 'making it' on their own terms, and that it's the attractiveness of these terms, and the success these women have made of them, that make them so inspiring to us now. This goes some way in explaining the continued fascination we have in reading and hearing about these women; through books, magazines and the media as well as the increasing numbers of women's networks and support groups.

All of the individual stories and journeys here are unique, but each of these women shares a common purpose: to make something of themselves, to make a positive difference, and to educate other women as well as their own children to be the best that they can be. Those women with daughters want to ensure they are positive role models. Most experience guilt in spending time at the office but many also say that, with hindsight, their children have benefited in the long run. They have become more independent, inspired and aspirational.

Many of the interviewees are remarkably similar in their outlook. Mary Perkins (Specsavers) and Karen Hanton (toptable.co.uk) are both devoted to their particular charities as well as progressing their particular sectors; Christian Rucker of The White Company and Glenda Stone of Aurora believe it's all about attention to detail, while Claire Locke (Artigiano), Debbie Moore (Pineapple) and Claire Burnet (Chococo) all founded their businesses around their particular passions in life – Italian fashion, dance and chocolate respectively.

The majority of those 'inspiring women' featured named Anita Roddick as the most powerful influence on women entrepreneurs and business as a whole, and almost all believed that several factors were key in being a successful entrepreneur:

- Watch your budget
- Do your research and know your market
- Be passionate about what you're doing
- Know your own limitations – do outsource if it makes business sense
- Don't underestimate the amount of hours involved
- Ask for advice and have good support systems
- Learn from your mistakes
- Know that good supplier relationships are key
- Take care of your staff
- Believe in yourself, have courage and confidence

Women today perhaps take for granted the fact that they have so many options open to them. If they choose to, they can work or stay at home. Some, for financial reasons, have to juggle both, while others decide that – for their own sanity – they need to do both. There's no black or white, right or wrong.

I myself wrote this book whilst pregnant with my second daughter. I hope the very act of fulfilling my own long-held ambition will offer my children both a mother and a role model.

We want to know how other women have done it. We want reassurance that it is possible. We want to be inspired. It is my sincere hope that this book does just that for you.

Michelle Rosenberg

Annabel Karmel MBE

'**I think I've become**', says Annabel Karmel MBE, 'a sort of guru for feeding children in this country.'

Hers is no idle boast. Annabel's hugely popular books on baby food and nutrition (she has written 14 with a 15th on its way) are something of a rite of passage for all mums anxious to feed their children properly.

Annabel never planned to become an author. In fact she originally trained as a musician, playing the harp professionally and performing with the likes of Liberace and Boy George; but it was her experiences as a mother that changed her life. Her first child, Natasha, died from a rare viral infection in 1987 when she was just three months old. 'It's not something you can ever come to terms with', says Annabel quietly. 'And it was probably the catalyst that got me into writing books.'

Annabel's second child, Nicholas, was an extremely fussy eater which made her feel vulnerable about his well-being. 'Probably more than any other mother, I wanted to make sure that he ate well. So, as a mum, I looked for a book on feeding babies. There was nothing! It was like "you poach some liver in milk and you purée it." It didn't taste very nice!'

Determined to provide her son with tasty and nutritious food, Annabel started experimenting with her own recipes. Her first guinea pigs were the other mums at the playgroup she ran in St. John's Wood as their children didn't eat very well either. They soon started trying Annabel's recipes and loved them, encouraging her to write a book. She sat on the idea for six months then realised it would be good therapy to help get over Natasha's death.

'At least I could give something back and help other children. I wrote it as therapy, for Natasha, in memory of her death. I never thought it would be a popular book. Baby food was the last subject you'd choose to be a best-seller. I couldn't find a publisher for a long time. Everybody turned it down.'

Rejected 15 times, she eventually got it published in 1991, and within three months *The Complete Baby and Toddler Meal Planner* had sold out. It went on to sell in 20 different countries, and from that day until now, it has consistently been in the top five best-selling cookery books in the UK. 'This book is 15 years old but in every single best-seller list, it's still there. It's phenomenal', says Annabel.

The book was the catalyst for the Annabel Karmel brand. For the next few years, she focused purely on writing, publishing a further 13 books including *Superfoods for Babies and Children, Top 100 Baby Purées, Complete Party Planner* and *Children's First Cookbook* with two more books out this year; *The Fussy Eaters Recipe Book* and a completely revised photographic edition of *The New Complete Baby and Toddler Meal Planner*.

Annabel is still bemused by the sheer scale of her success:

I don't know how it became like that but there was this need because mums had this problem with feeding their children. They didn't have someone they could trust and got so many different opinions from everybody on what was right to give their children. But what I did was to work with Great Ormond Street Hospital and the Institute of Child Health. I found out the real truth about feeding children and it's much more about common sense. Do give them lots of variety. Don't withhold giving them fish, meat and eggs; all these things are very

Annabel sampling her recipes

important to your child. You have this window of opportunity, between six and 12 months when they're actually pretty good eaters. But beyond that time, they can become pretty fussy. So try and get them to take as many foods as possible, because it will help them.

Once she'd got over the hurdle of publishing the first one, it got easier. 'I created a niche market which is very much mine', she says. 'Although people have brought out books on feeding children, I don't think they give them the love, care and attention that I do. I don't know anyone who tests recipes as much as I do, and then tests them on children again. I can't help it but I am a perfectionist in what I do.' There is one downside, however, which she wasn't quite prepared for. 'No-one invites me to dinner parties any more!' she laughs. 'They don't want to cook themselves, as they think I'm such a good cook!'

In the beginning, Annabel looked to her husband for business support and advice on contracts but in the last year, as the Annabel Karmel brand has grown and with the retail, licensing and branding deals pouring in, she realised that she needed to build up her own team of people. Annabel recruited a new business-development manager in January 2007 and now says she couldn't do without her. 'I'm terribly enthusiastic and can go off on a tangent', she says. 'She will rein me in and suggest where we should concentrate and the area in which we should be going.' Annabel also has someone handling her PR and a chairman of the company, who handles the finance.

When she made the decision to branch out and enter the food business, a friend lent her some money so she could start designing packaging and make appointments to meet supermarkets. She soon realised that in order to continue, she had to have a solid business plan in place.

A friend gave her a loan of a few hundred thousand pounds which she has now paid back with interest, and the rest she has funded through her book royalties. Anything Annabel earns from ad hoc promotional work for brands such as Tropicana and Rachel's Dairy also goes into the pot (although she is quick to point out that she does turn down opportunities. 'If someone like Smarties came to me and asked me to endorse a campaign, I would say no. I'll only do things I feel are right for the integrity of the brand.')

Annabel admits she did a huge amount of market research – investing around £50,000 – but she feels she made a mistake in waiting too long to embark on this stage of her business:

I felt that I couldn't do it by myself and I needed a big company behind me. But if I had my time again, I would have just done it. You always think that someone else can do it better than you can, but no one will give it the care, love and attention that I will. I test the recipes many, many times and I make sure that when it goes to the factory, it is of a quality I want it to be. I want to create a brand that mums can trust.

Boots were the first ones to approach Annabel. The 'Make Your Own' range currently includes food, drink and cooking equipment to help mums, and the aim, says Annabel, is to 'take the hard work away from the mum and help them to give their child the best start in life by giving them something fresh. Jars have a shelf life of two years and that wasn't the way to go. I felt very strongly that I wanted all babies to have completely fresh food. So this is it!' The food has done very well, which she says is 'remarkable', as Boots is not a food retailer.

In January 2007, Annabel launched into 130 Sainsbury's stores with her 'Eat Fussy' food range for young children; something that has now extended to 400 stores. 'I did this range myself', she says.

It took a while and I never thought I could do it. I went into the supermarkets myself to see what was going on and realised there was a huge gap in the market of this age range of one to four years. I tried all the food for 4+ that the supermarkets produced and they were very bland. It's very important to start them on the right basics and that's why I wanted to do it.

Role MODEL

I was related to Rosalind Franklin, the scientist who was largely responsible for the discovery of DNA, and she has always been a person who inspired me. She did not find life easy as a woman and a scientist and left a great legacy to mankind. She gave up her life for her work and died young. She was a great mentor for me in her passion for her work and for breaking new ground that has made such a difference to our lives.

The recipes apparently taste like home made, with titles for the mums such as 'Mummy's Favourite Fish Pie', 'Meatballs in Tomato Sauce with Spaghetti' and 'Hidden Vegetable Pasta'. The 'Eat Fussy' range is available at Ocado and in Co-op. Annabel is also looking to approach other supermarkets such as Tesco.

Having created a very loyal following through her books, Annabel has decided to grow her brand through licensing. Her aim is to find the best manufacturer in each of the product categories that she intends to enter, and she is currently developing food ranges with Greencore, one of Europe's leading food manufacturers.

When considering how she feels having major retailers call and put offers on the table, she shakes her head:

> It's unbelievable. I always find it strange how well known I've become. I speak to almost anyone who has a child and they've read my book or cooked my recipes and there is kind of a bond between me and every mum now because everyone has a favourite recipe or book. Some even make them for their dinner parties, not just for their child! What is nice is that the pages of my books are always covered with food which shows that they don't just sit on the shelf. Touching people's lives, making a difference to people's lives, is fantastic.

Annabel sources most of her food from British suppliers. 'As much as possible comes from this country', she says firmly. She describes her suppliers as the loveliest people; she has a great relationship with them and regards them as partners.

In recognition of the huge and growing interest in her brand, Annabel Karmel Group Holdings was established in 2006. The brand covers everything to do with food and equipment, and turnover for 2007 will be around the £5m mark. Projections for 2008 are £10m but it is too early to disclose profit.

Annabel has recently launched a range of innovative and stylish weaning products including bowls, cups, feeding spoons and bibs with Lindam, a leading manufacturer of baby goods. She has also recently taken her passion to the USA, explaining that 'they have a lot of problems with their children and obesity. Nobody has really captured this niche market in America. Their need is even greater than ours so I decided, off my own bat, that I would go and find a publisher.'

The impulse paid off. In 2006, she published four books with Simon & Schuster, and she has three more out in the US next year. She's just been signed up by the powerful talent agency, William Morris, and her aim is to now do more television, build up her profile and be able to do food and equipment over there.

It's only been very recently that Annabel has regarded herself as a true entrepreneur. Before that, she considered herself as just an author, but she's certainly not surprised to be where she is now. She's always had the vision of where she wanted to be, and that included a range of her own foods.

Her typical day sounds hectic but it's clear she thrives on the pace. As well as developing recipes for a new book and tasting recipes for her new range (which launched in Tootsies in September) there are marketing meetings, speaking to her PR about opportunities with pregnancy and parenting club Bounty – where she has provided a whole section on child nutrition – and reviewing her average morning inbox of 150 emails. When asked about her work/life balance, she laughs and says its mostly work, but she doesn't mind because she loves it.

I just work till 2 am in the morning until I finish. I'm always happy when I'm working. In order to get where I have, I've had to give up a huge amount of my social life. When I was younger I was a musician and I had to do the same thing; I had to practice. Other people went out to parties or sat down and watched television but I never did that. It's very unusual for me to be at home, sitting down, and not busy and working.

Now a mother of three, on reflection she says she consciously chose a profession where she could be at home as she wanted to be there for her family. 'For many women, sometimes it's difficult to be in business because you are a mother', she says, 'and that's probably why it's taken me so long, because

Advice to other
ENTREPRENEURS

If you're a mother, choose a profession which enables you to spend quality time with your children.

I wanted to be a good mother. So if you are like that, choose a profession where you can be with your kids and you don't have to be in an office until 9 pm.'

In June 2006, the Queen made Annabel Karmel a MBE for her outstanding work in the field of child nutrition, an honour she says that was totally unexpected. 'It was fantastic because it's nothing to do with being commercial; it's to do with changing people's lives. How did they find me? How did they dig me out of all the people? I have no idea. But it was very nice!'

Annabel would like to see improvements in the standard of food served to children in this country. She has her eye on theme parks like Alton Towers and Thorpe Park as well as restaurant chains like Little Chef, who recently approached her.

'Everybody I go to is incredibly enthusiastic about what I do', she says. 'The timing now couldn't be better. You only have to open a newspaper to read that 3.5 million people in the UK are suffering from malnutrition, because they eat junk food.'

She wants, in the future, to be campaigning for better food for younger children:

If I can improve the quality of food for children in this country, that's the best legacy I can ever have. Natasha helped me do that. I would never have done that without her being born. That's my aspiration. She had a short life but something good came out of it. I think this is probably what I'll do for the rest of my life. I feel I'm just starting; that everything I've done up until now has been for this beginning.

———— *JW* ————

Chrissie Rucker

That she is wearing a crisp white shirt is a given. The fact, however, that Christian (Chrissie) Rucker reveals she likes to let off steam listening to Robbie Williams, twice a week on her treadmill, is a little more unexpected. It's an endearing confession from the founder of a multi-million-pound, multi-channel retail company with 500 staff, 17 stores and sales this year on track to be in excess of £70m.

A former assistant beauty editor at *Harper's & Queen*, Chrissie started The White Company in August 1993 because she couldn't find all the basics she wanted to buy for her boyfriend – Charles Tyrwitt Shirts founder Nick Wheeler's – flat in white:

Why white? Initially I was shopping for Nick for his home, buying bed linen and towels. Those are just the things that I personally love to have in white.

And because I was a journalist, I knew there had to be a good hook for the business; that selling all white things would really separate us from other people. The great thing about white is that it is incredibly versatile – whether country or penthouse, there is always a place for white. It has a very broad appeal.

With Nick's encouragement, she decided to pursue the idea and supply her products via mail order. 'When I started this business', she says, 'I set myself a very clear deadline. I was 24 when I started and I thought, I'll do this for a year and if it works, great, if not I'll just get myself another job. But I did set myself a time span.'

Chrissie did a lot of market research and found her previous journalistic, PR and fashion design experience a distinct advantage. 'I rang up quite a few of the department stores, pretending I was writing an article for someone, and said "could you tell me what percentage of your bed linen sales are white?" I think having a magazine and journalistic background was phenomenal.'

She invested £20,000 of her own money and made use of £50 a week from CENTEC, the Hammersmith and Fulham business grant scheme. She then spent the latter part of that year securing suppliers and putting together her first 12-page brochure, which featured bed linen and towels. Working on a very tight budget, she used her editorial experience to write a press release to introduce The White Company to the shopping and home editors of the leading newspapers and magazines. A week before the official launch, the *Financial Times* ran with the story – her hunch about the 'white' news hook had been spot on. The journalists and her first customers loved the story, the concept and, most crucially, the products.

For the first six months, Chrissie ran the business out of a room in Nick's house. She and Nick's sister logged, packed and delivered orders themselves with just a phone, fax and computer. The White Company turned a profit in its first year.

With business booming, The White Company looked for its first retail outlet and opened in London's Chelsea in 2001. Chrissie was very much involved in setting up the brand and, inspired by examples she'd seen in the USA, knew how she wanted her own first store to look. She always had a natural feel for what products would work; from duvets and pillows to table linen, accessories, glassware, and bath products. 'It's very instinctive', she says. 'It's just there. I have very strong views about what I like and don't like.'

A White Company bedroom

Originally she would do all the buying trips herself; travelling to Egypt, India, Portugal, Italy and France. 'The beauty of it', she says, 'is that the product comes in but you don't pay for it until 30 days later. It's all about the timing. You're selling all the time which brings in the revenue to pay for the product.' And when it comes to product, Chrissie is obsessive about quality and value.

'I think that's what we've always really focused on. What we do is work directly with the factories, cutting out the middleman. We're producing high-quality products at high-street prices. That's the heart of what the company is all about.'

Unsurprisingly, she says good relationships with suppliers are crucial and encourages reciprocal visits as often as possible; 'if you don't have a fantastic relationship with your supplier, you don't have a product', she says.

Chrissie says her biggest challenge was keeping up with the rapid growth of the business; 'we've consistently grown incredibly quickly which has been wonderful – but quite often you find that you are firefighting because you are growing so fast that you're peddling to keep up with it all. You have phases where it gets really difficult and challenging.' She also admits to having made mistakes. 'We make little mistakes the whole time', she acknowledges. 'You just learn from them. In the early days, the mistakes were with the suppliers we first used. I've always seen that as a positive thing as you learn from them each time. If we make a mistake with a customer, we're very upfront and do whatever we can to make it right.'

The only thing Chrissie misses from the early days of the business is not having her dogs in the office. It seems they got a little too 'messy' for the rest of her staff.

When you start, you're a very small, tight team and you have this fantastic very close-knit, family-feel environment. That is something we have tried to keep even whilst we get bigger. I'm not someone who looks back. I look forward. I wouldn't change anything for the world because it's all been part of the process.

Whilst her management team has expanded, Chrissie is still heavily involved in every aspect of the business. She oversees the promotion cards, marketing team and production of the regularly updated brochures (there's a new one mailed every eight weeks) which she personalises by writing all the intros and the tips that accompany them. She's also responsible for the overall look and feel of the stores.

Chrissie believes it is crucial to be utterly passionate about what you want to do. 'Believe in it 200%. You have to be commercial; you have to know there is a genuine market for what you want to sell. You need to do your homework on that and be very sure that the idea is valid and that enough people will want it. Once you know that, just go for it.'

Product development is Chrissie's own passion. Even as the business has grown and changed, it has always been very personal to her and her life. She explains:

There is not ever any part of my life where I'm not influenced by The White Company. For example, we were recently on holiday (in Antigua) but the whole time we were away, I was looking at the furniture around me. I'm like this kind of mad woman – just being on the beach and watching what everyone is wearing. I sketch the whole time and, if I can, take pictures. I'm constantly trying to look for the next thing. My main role is just championing the brand, keeping it on track and not letting it drift – making sure we are sticking by our core brand philosophies.

Chrissie has a top team of seven, together with a managing director who runs the business side. She says it's essential for a founder to acknowledge their strengths and delegate responsibilities accordingly: 'you have to surround yourself with people who are great at the things you are hopeless at. That is what I've tried to do. I'm not a numbers person at all, I'm definitely product.'

In keeping with Chrissie's fastidious attention to detail, The White Company is all about providing superb customer service as it's something she's very aware of as a consumer herself:

The other day, I was in the linen department of a leading department store and the salesman made me feel 'this' high. He looked at me, guided me away from the expensive area that I was looking at and said 'madam, I think you may be more interested in this' it was such a classic example of really bad customer service. So it is terribly important to me that when people come into the store that they are made to feel welcome and that we're there to help them when they're ready for help. We're not going to be pushy or try to oversell to them but just give them space.

Role **MODEL**

I really admire Estée Lauder and love the fact she has kept her amazing business in the family! My husband, Nick Wheeler, my MD Patricia Burnett and my Chairman Tony Campbell.

Chrissie invests a lot in her staff training programmes, personally visiting the store, popping in unannounced and conducting mystery shopping to score the stores on how they are doing. 'I always try to make my visits in store as positive as possible. If something's not right, I'll just go and speak to the manager – I know all the managers really well anyway', she says. 'We're arming them with the knowledge that they can then just go in and confidently deliver what we hope is the brand experience that we're trying to give. If you don't arm them with the equipment, you can't blame them if they don't react or treat people in the way you'd like them to.'

She knows she couldn't be a stay at home mum but believes her happiness and fulfilment from her work life reflect positively on her children:

I absolutely love my children to pieces – they're our lives. But I just love working. I always have; I love having the passions and challenges that come every day. I love the people in the office, I love coming here every day and I love being at work. I try really hard to get a balance and good quality time with the children, and really exciting, challenging work. The combination of the two is fantastic. It is exhausting at times but you learn to manage that over time. I'm only in the office three days a week now. On Mondays and Fridays, I work from home. I do the school run, I have lunch with my little daughter when she's at home for lunch, I'm there at teatime when they come home, I can bath them and see them do their homework. One of the great advantages in having your own business is that you can do that.

There has never been a time when she thought she has 'made it.' Getting complacent, she believes, is a recipe for disaster. Instead, she says she drives her team 'bonkers' in her pursuit of perfection, explaining:

We'll create something new and that will be lovely and we'll be really excited about it. But when we've done that, I want to go on and do the next version of it and I want it to be even better. So I'm always pushing. I'm always looking to improve, enhance. You have to keep moving forward and keep lots of freshness. I'm just constantly looking for new things and new ways to get better.

Keeping it 'fresh' means continually expanding and diversifying their product range, something that can be seen in the launch of two franchises in Dubai and the opening of The Little White Company for children.

Husband Nick is still a director of the business and has always had a huge and guiding influence on Chrissie. 'We are a complete pair of "saddos"', she laughs.

> *We talk shop at home but we both love it. The lovely thing about it is that there are so many similarities between the two businesses; he will help me interview someone if I'm not sure about them and I'll do the same for him; we have very different skill sets but we complement each other. Nick is very much an operator and a financial person, whereas I'm much more of a creative, look and feel person. If my husband did something completely different, did a regular nine-to-five job, it would be a disaster. Every Sunday evening we'll both be sitting at our desks getting emails ready for the next day. The great thing is that we manage to get time off together for the children, proper family time. Because we're in the same situation, it works.*

Advice to other ENTREPRENEURS

Believe in your idea. Ensure there is a market for it. Do your homework and go for it!

Chrissie adores her job and the regular challenges its presents. She says her four children, Tom (10), Ella (9), India (7) and Bea (3), are her proudest achievement but that she is just as pleased to watch the progression of her team over the years:

> *I love the fact that five years ago I watched people in this business come in, doing one job, and I look at what they're doing now, how they've grown, changed and developed. We all learn together. We all get better at our jobs. Its lovely to see the business growing and the excitement that goes with it.*

Currently working on the company's five-year plan, Chrissie believes The White Company has the potential to be an international brand. She hopes to be a £100m pound business by 2010 and would love to get into the US market but adds:

I think we have much more to do here first. I do not want a White Company on every high street. I don't want it to lose its boutique-ness and to become a Body Shop or Gap. I want it to remain special. I'm probably just somebody who started something that I really believed in and I still love doing it. I have no intentions of stopping or trying to start a new business. I'm just very happy carrying along and growing and developing this business.

Chrissie Rucker is nothing if not self-deprecating. 'I think I have become the guest from hell', she acknowledges ruefully:

I realised that when we went to stay at a skiing chalet. I am so fussy about how it feels when you get into bed and I felt the bed was uncomfortable; the pillows were really lumpy; the sheets were quite nice but the duvets were horrible. I think probably one of the things people always say when they come and stay with us is that they get into bed and it's just heaven. I suppose my mission is to give everybody the most comfortable bed they can possibly have. So what is my favourite product? Anything that makes the bed feel perfect, probably.

——————— *JW* ———————

CHOCOCO

THE PURBECK CHOCOLATE CO.

Claire Burnet

Claire **Burnet is not** your average chocoholic. By her own apologetic admission, she is bordering on 'evangelical' when it comes to talking about her consuming passion.

Together with husband Andy, mother-of-two Claire set up Chococo: The Purbeck Chocolate Company, in 2002, with the aim of being an ethical chocolate maker. It was a move brought about by their general disillusionment with their corporate lives in marketing (Claire ex-Shell UK Oil, Procter & Gamble and Disney Channel) and finance (ex-Andersons and United Biscuits accountant Andy).

'Andy was increasingly unhappy commuting from Hammersmith to the City as a finance director for a software company. We didn't see ourselves living in London long term with a family. I also had the burning desire to build my own brand that I would be proud of', says Claire.

They upped sticks and moved to Swanage in Purbeck, Dorset, with their young daughter, Lily. The impulse was in keeping with Claire's mantra that 'life is not a dress rehearsal', although the area wasn't completely new to them – they'd got married there in 1999.

Their inspiration was driven in part by Claire's love of chocolate, her 'foodie' mother and the fact that her parents had lived in Brussels whilst she was a student. 'When I used to go back to see them', she remembers, 'we would eat fabulous fresh chocolates handmade by local artisan chocolatiers.'

The launch of their company happily coincided with an increase in UK consumer interest in what Claire calls the 'provenance' of food – where it comes from and how it is produced. Most personally, perhaps, the business came about from Claire's own poor experiences with British 'premium' chocolate. 'I got tired of working on other people's brands. I knew the time was right', she says of the decision to set up her own.

Using the money they raised by selling their flat in London, they bought an old hairdressing salon and remodelled it to encompass a chocolate workshop on the ground floor and the shop upstairs. They invested £75,000 in setting it up.

Whilst Claire says it has taken three years to make a profit, she admits they haven't seen much of it. 'We are always investing back into the business; paying staff, building stock, investing in new moulds and packaging, and not paying ourselves', she admits wryly.

Aside from a chocolate-making course in Yorkshire, the rest of the business was learnt on the job. Their first shop fittings were their dining room table and some antique furniture Andy had inherited.

Claire says their biggest challenge was 'the vertical learning curve in both making chocolates and selling them without a huge budget to employ staff and kit out our shop properly', but doggedly, they persevered. Claire designed the packaging with Pearlfisher, a London design company whose owners live in Purbeck, and together Claire and Andy worked to ensure their products were, ethically and ingredient-wise, the real chocolate deal.

They did their homework through an exhaustive variety of channels; 'we researched the premium and overall chocolate market via online searches, site visits, ordering competitor products and talking to industry suppliers', says Claire. They read as much as they could and researched the local market in terms of demographics, visitor numbers and spending patterns from tourist data and visiting farmers' markets.

Chocolate creations from Chococo

After preparing a business plan, they approached a number of banks, looking to set up a business account. However, after finding the services of the one whose help they had enlisted 'hopeless' they eventually switched to another bank, which offered them the benefits of a local business manager.

Whilst they named their business The Purbeck Chocolate Company after the region in which it is based, it was 'a bit of a mouthful' and they settled on Chococo, which comes from the 'choco' of chocolate and the 'co' of company, as being slightly easier to digest.

They use fine-origin chocolate with known provenance, and local Dorset produce, including the fresh cream for their ganaches (a blend of chocolate and cream). And when they can't go local, they try to source ethically produced ingredients.

Their working roles are refreshingly non-traditional. Andy has become the chief chocolate maker (Claire says he has fallen in love with the science of chocolate and its tempering process, and has a 'wonderful eye for piping'). Claire takes care of most of the business side of things, from marketing and PR to website design and product development. Whilst all decisions are 'pretty much' made jointly, Claire has been on the receiving end of some gender stereotypes:

> *I have had the phone put down on me when men have rung asking to speak to the owner and I have said, 'Speaking!' Sometimes I get the sense that some of our agency contacts assume that Andy makes all the decisions and I am just 'playing' at being a partner. I am aware of having to modify my style in situations more than Andy has to, as my involved, passionate approach doesn't always go down well in more masculine environments.*

The fresh-cream chocolates (currently numbering 34, amongst a total range of around 85 creations) have been given names Willy Wonka would have been proud of and are reminiscent of an old-fashioned sweet shop: Lemon Zing, Raspberry Riot, Chilli tickle, Totally Tonka and Apple Dilly.

'If you don't have a palette you can forget it', says Claire, 'because you can make a lot of abominable chocolates and think they taste fantastic, and they don't. It is easy to allow flavours to overpower and get the overall balance wrong. There are some flavours that I knew I wanted to do and others where we took a classic flavour combination and turned it on its head.' A classic example of this is their raspberry truffle rolled in crushed dried raspberries. 'Now others are doing it!' she says.

Their determination not to use any additives or preservatives in their chocolates means that Chococo products last around two weeks.

'Rather than be frightened of that, we're proud', she says. 'It makes it hard, because we're always making and at Christmas, when we do the bulk of our mail-order business, it's a key time, and because everyone wants gifts, we cannot make them ahead. We have to make them, pack them and dispatch them, often within 24-hour periods because they only have a short shelf life.'

It means Claire and Andy's team of four full timers, seven part timers and extra seasonal staff, work round the clock. 'It's a complete brain-draining exercise to make sure we've got the stocks right', she admits.

Chococo knew they had made an impact when *The Sunday Times Style* magazine's food writer Lydia Slater rang her in the summer of 2003. 'She was asking for a sample box as all her team had eaten the one we had sent whilst she was on holiday and demanded that she get one to try!' Indeed, even the environmental health officer who came to check them out when they first got going ended up making chocolates with them. 'He had a lovely time', laughs Claire.

With hindsight, Claire says they would have done certain things differently. 'We should have thought bigger upfront – we could have bought a bigger space initially but didn't think we would need it! We were also very naïve about the ease of finding staff with strong work ethics in a small town', she says.

Originally, they only opened their shop three afternoons a week. They are now open six days a week, and whilst they could be open seven, Claire is firm about their Sunday 'non-opening policy'. 'We've got kids, most of our staff have got kids, and some element of work/life balance is very important', she says.

They rapidly grew out of their space but were able to secure an upstairs space next to the shop, which became their packing area. 'Then', says Claire, 'we managed to acquire – across the alleyway from where we started – a store room, which we converted into a new larger factory in 2005. But it's still too small!' she laughs.

Role MODEL

Kristina Murrin, an old colleague of mine from Procter & Gamble, who manages to combine running a business, writing, developing a TV career, three children and a razor-sharp intellect in a very personal, friendly, down-to-earth manner! Glenda Stone who runs Aurora for her passion for encouraging women to succeed in whatever they want to achieve in business and Sir Chay Blyth who created the BT Global Challenge round the world yacht races inspired by his own solo round-the-world feat back in 1971. He taught me that 'persistence and determination are omnipotent'.

Fresh out of a meeting with Selfridges, Claire says that their young business, established in 2002, is also stocked in Harvey Nichols and other boutique retailers such as Villandry and Tom's Deli.

'Pretty much everyone that we supply approached us. They'd either seen us in other stores or they'd seen us in the press', says Claire. But she's at pains to point out that retailers are not her core business. 'The bulk of our business is direct to consumer. Our corporate and wedding businesses are growing well, but our online mail order – a quarter of the business – is growing the fastest.'

'We've turned down Fortnum & Masons', she says, 'and we've also turned down Gü, because they want to sell our chocolates under their branding, and we've just said no as it's not what we're about.' What they *are* about is 'turning the established paradigm of making chocolates with a long shelf life on its head.'

Claire is proud of using 'only fresh local ingredients, origin chocolate with known provenance' (no 'Belgian' chocolate here) and not using any additives or preservatives. In May 2007 and testament to how seriously they take their 'local produce' credentials, Chococo became full members of Direct from Dorset, an origin assurance scheme run by Dorset County Council which assures consumers they are buying products sourced from and made in Dorset.

Claire is reticent about revealing too much of their profits. 'There's lots of interest in the market and what we're up to', she explains. 'It's a very dynamic market at the moment with lots of new entrants coming in, and we're having discussions about how we grow within that.'

Her advice to any women looking to set up in business is not to do it on their own. 'You need support networks!' she says. 'It's a lonely business running your own business and being a mum. I have yet to make many good friends locally, and if it wasn't for Andy's previous connections with the town helping us settle in, I would have found it even tougher.'

She admits working with her husband is an intense experience:

We do wind each other up sometimes as we don't hold formal meetings in the way normal business partners would do. We often end up trying to resolve important issues late at night when we are tired – bad idea! However, we have very different personalities and skill sets so it does work overall. You have to be disciplined, try not to get tired at the same time and have time out. One of the benefits, though, is that Andy is getting to spend more time with the kids than he ever would have done if we had carried on with our old lives.

Advice to other **ENTREPRENEURS**

If you are also a mum, don't do it alone – get support!

Juggling work and family, Claire says she hopes she is doing the right thing for her two children and will be able to spend more time with them as the business becomes more established. 'I also hope that they see 'mum' as someone who has a life beyond just being their mum and that that is inspirational.'

Whilst awards for Chococo include a 'Highly Commended' Finalist in the Waitrose Small Producers Award in 2006, as well as a 2003 packaging design award, Claire says her proudest achievements are winning 18 fine-food awards, especially, the gold, silver and bronze medals in the Academy of Chocolate Awards in 2005.

'That was a great achievement for us, given the stiff competition amongst the best chocolatiers in the UK', she says.

Perhaps surprisingly, when surrounded by chocolate 24/7, Claire says she never tires of eating it. 'Absolutely not! I am totally addicted to the point where if I don't eat any during the day, I have a secret stash at home.'

Claire believes that combining dual passion for ethics and business is a growing trend, especially for women. It certainly applies to her vision for Chococo:

Success is not about getting funding to mass produce our chocolates for mass distribution everywhere. Which means it's going to be hard, because we're going to do it on our own terms. I have friends who say 'why don't you just outsource that – get someone else to do it.' No! We make all our chocolates ourselves so that we can own the process. We know where all the ingredients come from. When we say they're handmade, they are genuinely handmade. When we say they're fresh, they're genuinely fresh. It's completely open and transparent. We're real people making real chocolates in a real place. It's absolutely integral to what we're about.

Claire passionately believes that fine chocolate should be for everyone.

> *We're not a very chi-chi, designer boutique. We are family-friendly. If customers want to come into our shop and buy a 25p chocolate dinosaur for their kids, that's absolutely fine. If they want to spend a lot of money on boxes of fresh truffles, that's absolutely fine as well. We're not intimidating in a way that a lot of premium chocolate is.*

———————— *JW* ————————

ARTIGIANO
Claire Locke

La Dolce Vita! Claire Locke has about 28 million reasons to relish her personal mantra 'if you fail, try again!' The founder of Italian fashion mail-order specialist Artigiano recently sold the business she founded with husband Glyn in 1995. 'This is where the story is good and interesting for other women', says Claire, 'because it does show that you can do it.'

Born in Shropshire in 1960, Claire's love affair with all things Italian stemmed from the teenage summers she and her sister shared with an exchange family on the Ligurian coast. No one spoke English. She had no choice but to learn Italian and develop her passion for its fashion.

Italian women always looked fabulous; always in the current style, beautifully groomed and elegantly dressed. I was intrigued to find out how they did it.

All I ever wanted to do was to import clothes from Italy. I didn't have this mission to convert British women to copies of Italian women – it was more about sharing a wonderful discovery.

She studied PPE (philosophy, politics and economics) at Oxford before marrying young love, Glyn, and joining him in his rowing-boat business. Working together would prove a good trial run for the couple.

After a couple of years Claire realised her true ambitions and enthusiasm lay elsewhere and in 1984 she launched Scala Collections, acting as a UK agent for some high-profile Italian manufacturers. She supplied groups such as Austin Reed, Selfridges and Aquascutum.

'That's how I learnt the business', she says, 'By being a supplier to big groups.'

I went out there on my own, found some manufacturers and somehow persuaded them to give me a chance. Then I went over there and they taught me everything they knew, and I got on with it. I used the usual Italian method of 'friends of friends' in finding the best people to talk to. There's no such thing as cold-calling in Italy!

After eight years, and a family move with her two young sons to the Isle of Wight, Claire decided it was time to branch out on her own and sell via mail-order catalogue. The timing couldn't have been better – the industry was just becoming exciting, and Claire knew she'd have a niche place in the market.

Artigiano, meaning 'artisan', started from their kitchen table. The aim was to produce a catalogue which would have the feel of a high-end fashion magazine and provide the very best of Italian style. Says Claire:

I remember having all the pictures all over the table. We did have a very loose business plan but we very quickly had to prepare a proper one. It's very important to have one because its only when you go through that plan, and you particularly work out your cash flow and how much capital you will need, that you will really get to grips with whether you can fund it.

They spent £1,000 on a small advertisement in the back pages of fashion bible *Vogue*. Business boomed, mostly through word of mouth.

Italians do it better! An Artigiano catalogue

Initially they managed on their own funds and an overdraft, which at one point reached a couple of hundred thousand pounds. After three years, they raised money through 3-i, one of the biggest venture capital companies in the UK and sold them part of the company, before buying them out again out a few years later.

Like anyone building a database from scratch, it cost Claire and Glyn more to recruit a customer than the profit they gained from selling to that customer. Explains Claire: 'the business only becomes profitable when you have enough repeat customers buying again to subsidise the expansion. We didn't make a profit for three years – that's a long time to finance.'

Claire admits things didn't always go smoothly. 'I don't think there's any buyer who hasn't made mistakes, and that would include me. One of the secrets of our success is the fantastic relationships we have with our suppliers in Italy – the core suppliers are the same people I worked with 20 years ago.'

She credits husband Glyn for propelling the business forward:

When we ran out of computer space or needed a new warehouse, he'd be the one who'd do the project. Thank goodness I never had to and he sorted those things out. He was also incredibly good on the strategy. He tends to be quite general and I am very detailed and specific; between the two of us, we were very good foils of each other.

As the business grew, with its focus on style and quality of service, she admits her husband deserves the credit for taking the business online, saying 'it's exactly the kind of thing that he was always incredibly far-sighted about. We registered artigiano.com way back in 1997 and were one of the first companies to have a website and then a transactional website. Compared to our competitors, we have a very high level of internet usage.'

Whilst a working marriage worked for them, Claire wouldn't recommend it for everyone:

It is difficult; your home and work life gets hopelessly blurred. You try and have rules like 'we're not going to talk about work before 9am' – it just doesn't work. You talk about it 24 hours, seven days a week. Having said that, it does give you a certain lifestyle. You can organise it so that your children are picked up from school. You can take your holidays together; you have that trust between you that if one says they'll do it, you believe they will. In a normal business partnership, you may have some concern that that may not be the case. If you have a robust enough relationship and you're able to ignore what's work, it can work.

Claire's focus, and the area of the business she loves most, was product for the collections. 'We produce over 20 catalogues a year', she says, 'it really is a relentless programme in terms of sourcing, photographing, mailing and fulfilling. It's quite a number!'

She also had the added day-to-day pressure of running the business.

> *Role* **MODEL**
>
> My greatest mentor has always been my father who had an outstanding business career and upon retirement became chairman of Artigiano. His clarity of thought and support during the difficult periods were invaluable.

When you're growing fast, it's incredibly exciting. Our first Christmas party, there were four of us, and then eight, 16, 32, 64…it was really like that. You buy a telephone system and you just get it in and working, and within a year you have to replace it because it is not big enough anymore. And it's the same with your computer system and your premises. I remember one time when the whole ground floor of our house had to be cleared to put stock in because we'd run out of space. Eventually we built this state-of-the-art warehouse, which is where everything is now; but when you grow, there are space needs, equipment needs and the people. Recruiting enough people quickly enough, and training them quickly enough, is hugely time-consuming.

Claire recalls the incredible buzz of excitement and how there was never a moment when she stood still. Up until 2006, she would be away at hotels for four months of the year doing photo shoots and buying trips. With new issues and challenges presenting themselves on an almost daily basis, she says it takes courage to make a success of any business.

Obviously you can reduce your mistakes by talking to other people as much as possible first, which is what we did. Also, with my background in economics, I didn't find it daunting or difficult. I had always been interested in mail order. I loved the whole logistics of it. I wrote some of the first computer programs myself; you've got to be brave and give it a go. Just because you've never had the experience of doing something doesn't mean you shouldn't do it.

Claire never actively sought to promote herself, preferring to keep a low profile. You will never find her photograph in a catalogue, and she admits she's not a great publicity seeker:

In fact my husband has got cross with me on various occasions because he thinks if I did adopt a higher profile, it would have done the business a lot of good, but that's just how I am. I've always been much more interested in promoting the brand and what the catalogue stands for than in trying to sound like I'm very clever.

Despite shying away from the media, in November 2004 Claire was named Business Person of the Year by the Isle of Wight Chamber of Commerce. Artigiano has also won the coveted ECMOD Best Catalogue Award.

Claire's only real regret is the time she missed out with her family. Her sons were four and six when Claire started Artigiano and 16 and 18 when it was sold.

People say you're lucky that it only took 12 years, but it was the 12 years of my children's childhood. I live on the Isle of Wight, and most people have the summer off, go down to the beach and play tennis. I could never do any of those things because I was fully committed to the business. I'm sad about that, but you can't have your cake and eat it.

However, Claire is pleased that it made her sons independent and business savvy.

We used to talk about business at home – they have an incredibly good grasp of how businesses are started, built up, and now – how they are sold. It's been a great learning curve for them, we're still incredibly close and I don't think anyone's damaged. It's only me who feels a bit of regret. Everyone else is fine.

With its 130 staff based on the Isle of Wight, the business looks set to meet its target of £20m turnover by 2008. But Claire always had her eyes on the finishing line: an exit plan. 'The thing about having your own business – it's fantastic, thrilling and it gives you a huge buzz', she says.

'But, particularly if you are growing, expanding and changing and you're in a competitive industry, it's utterly all consuming. I had done it for 12 years, wanted a change and wanted to move on.'

Advice to other ENTREPRENEURS

If you fail, try, try, try again, and always strive for excellence.

In December 2006, Claire's solution was to support her 'talented and ambitious' management team in a MBO (management buyout), whereby she would still have a role moving forward, but not an executive one.

Dagmar Krafft, initially hired by Claire as a general manager, became the company's chief executive.

'What's important about creating a successful business', says Claire, 'is realising that it's not about you; it's about your next layer, the team underneath you.'

The purchase was backed by a private equity firm which retained a 65% stake, leaving Claire, Glyn and its management team holding on to the remaining 35%. Claire remains as a non-executive director.

'The whole point about being non-exec', she says, 'is that you don't do anything on a day-to-day basis. I have done so for the last few months, because I have been doing a handover to the new buying director. But once the handover is complete, I will be working with the board on strategic issues so the company can grow as fast as it can in the future.'

Claire says whilst she's not rushing out to start another business, she doesn't rule it out for the future:

> While I would be quite interested in becoming a business angel, where you invest in other start-up businesses, I haven't rushed off in order to start again at this stage. I've always had a very strong interest in business and am sure I will end up doing something. Nobody believes I'm going to retire, but we'll see!

And of the most important lesson she takes with her? The Italian phrase, *fare bella figura*. 'It means to do the right thing', she explains. 'The whole thing about doing business with Italy is that it's to do with trust, friendships, relationships, honour and keeping to your word. That's always how I've done business.'

When asked what defines a true entrepreneur, she considers the question thoughtfully. 'Someone', she says, 'who starts things from scratch, who achieves things against the odds and who is very resourceful. When you start a business you don't have an impressive business card or loads of money or power to get things done so you really have to persuade people to believe in you and want to help you. I think to that extent, yes, I did that.'

THE
STOPGAP
GROUP

Claire Owen

Claire **Owen never** thought very highly of recruitment consultants. Nor did it cross her mind that she would ever become one. So when she accidentally did in 1993, it took her two years before she would admit it to anyone (other than those closest to her!)

Fourteen years on, as the leader of The SG Group, she is now running an award-winning marketing and HR recruitment firm and has achieved her ambition of founding a firm that does things differently. The company has revenues in excess of £26m a year, around 120 staff, offices in London and Sydney and clients that include Nestlé, News International, Lloyds TSB, The Walt Disney Company, Sony and the NSPCC.

The conception of The SG Group, originally called Stopgap, was entirely unplanned. Claire, aged 30, had just given birth to her first child when her maternity leave came to an abrupt halt because her employer, a sales promotion agency, went bust. When made redundant, not only did Claire find herself thrown in the deep end, but so did several of her ex-clients left in the lurch with no agency to complete their marketing campaigns. Claire and a colleague, Gaynor Egan (who remained Claire's business partner for the next five years), approached one of these, Xerox, proposing they finish outstanding work on a freelance basis. Claire in effect provided them with a 'stopgap' solution and herself with a new business concept.

It soon became clear that while other professions had an established structure to providing temporary staff – such as locums to cover for doctors – there was a gaping hole in the marketing business. There was, as such, a golden opportunity to make a market for freelance marketing talent and to create the UK's first recruitment agency for freelance marketeers to exploit: Stopgap.

Keeping overheads low, Claire and Gaynor borrowed office space, a desk, computer and telephone, and conducted candidate interviews in a borrowed boardroom. 'If I'd needed £25,000 worth of capital and stock, it would have been a very different scenario', says Claire. 'But the way I saw it, I had a four-week-old baby and no job. Going out and getting a job would mean no control over my destiny and no flexibility, so logic said – let's try this. I could start to generate revenue straight away. I saw it as no risk – a no brainer. I'd always had a drive in me and I knew I'd be better working for myself than someone else so it seemed like the perfect opportunity.'

Everything was done on a tight budget with just a few hundred pounds spent on business cards, stationery and a black and white advertisement in the trade magazine *Marketing Week* to find freelancers.

'Everyone', says Claire, 'approaches their business in a different way. I was very cautious. Cost control and cash flow were key because I didn't want to borrow money. For the first years of the business, we didn't borrow any – we had no overdraft, debt, nothing.'

In the early days candidate records were kept manually on an Excel spreadsheet, and using what she learned in her business degree, Claire initially did the accounts herself. 'At least I knew what a P&L and a balance sheet looked like', she recalls. 'I used to say to Gaynor "OK, we have enough money in the bank – if we get no more business, we'll survive for a month." That was my own simple cash flow system. When we got to "if we get no more business, we can survive for six months," I knew we were OK. It was clear the business would keep coming in.'

An SG Group awayday, March 2006

They found clients using their network of agency contacts and sent out new business letters to marketing directors. Good timing and a lucky break brought them their first client, placing a German-speaking marketeer. One year in, they had around 500 candidates on their books, and having earned £60,000 in fees, they paid each other a salary of £10,000.

From the start, Claire was keen to do business differently from other recruitment agencies. Other agencies typically charged clients a mark up of 20 – 30% on what their temporary staff were paid. In a bold gamble, Claire asked her clients to put Stopgap candidates on their own payroll and pay Stopgap 15% of the total wage. The move paid off for both cash flow and marketing. Eventually, Claire set up Stopgap's own payroll system using an idiot's guide to running a payroll from the Inland Revenue.

When it came to interviewing potential freelance candidates, Claire also did things differently. With no training on how to conduct an interview, she relied on her gut instinct to draw candidates out and discover what made them tick – a process which turned out to be win–win for both client and candidate.

Her instincts also proved well founded when it came to hiring Stopgap's first two members of staff (one of whom is still with the company today). Claire says the first hires are one of the hardest recruitment tasks you'll ever make because to potential employees you are a 'risky option.'

If you're trying to recruit someone from scratch it can be extremely difficult and you can often resort to taking the best of a bad bunch. My advice, no matter whether it's your first employee or your 101st, is never compromise. You will always regret it. I always advocate a no compromise policy on recruitment; it will be one less business issue for you to have to worry about.

Claire's aversion to 'traditional' recruitment agencies fuelled her passion to make Stopgap a different breed of recruitment company, delivering an honest and ethical service to clients and candidates alike. 'We did advertise', explains Claire, 'but there was never any hard selling to candidate or clients. There's always a reminder in the marketing press that we're here but now, as in the early days, probably 40 – 50% of our business still comes through recommendations and word of mouth.'

Claire has always recruited her consultants from marketing roles rather than from other recruitment agencies for their understanding of clients' businesses, their needs and their experience of working in the marketing industry:

I'm still amazed when I talk with other recruiters and listen to what they do – counting how many new business calls their consultants make and how they earn commission. Our consultants don't earn commission – even if I'd known at the start that was how everyone else did things, I probably wouldn't have changed what I've done.

Her approach came as a breath of fresh air to cynical clients and candidates alike. By 1997, Stopgap had found work for around 2000 candidates, bought their own premises – Fitzroy House in Richmond, London – and grown to a staff of 16, seven of whom are still with the company today.

Claire is passionate about people, and the longevity and loyalty of her colleagues are testament to her determination to create a company that cares just as much about its employees as it does its customers. She believes that you are only as good as the people you employ and, as in any relationship, you have to invest time and energy for it to thrive. She had a clear vision of the working environment she wanted – one that she herself would like; social, comfortable and non-competitive.

'I just wanted it to be an extraordinarily nice place to work and an extraordinarily nice business to do business with', she says. 'A lot of the people that are with us are here because they want to work in an environment where they are trusted, not micromanaged, and it makes the people that we employ effective.'

Today, The SG Group's commitment to its staff is exemplary, with flexible working practices and benefits that include birthday and Christmas presents, free beer and wine at the end of the day, subsidised massage and reflexology, a lively social calendar, company-supported charity events and several team-building 'awaydays' each year.

The Awards the company has garnered speak for themselves: it was featured in the *Financial Times* top 10 Best Workplaces in 2006 and 2007 and Claire won the Special Award for Gender in both years, too. The company was in the top 15 *Sunday Times* Best Small Companies for four

Role MODEL

While there are quite a number of people I have worked with over the years that I certainly think of as inspiring, there is not one person who I'd feel comfortable highlighting over and above the others.

consecutive years and Claire is the only leader to be in the top three for *The Sunday Times'* Best Leadership Award for four years running; winning the award in 2005 and 2006.

Claire says that consideration for her staff is one of her core principles. She doesn't do anything without first considering the impact – emotional as well as commercial – it has on others. Claire lives her life like she runs her business, doing what she believes to be right rather than following what others do. She was genuinely delighted when one employee said they valued her leadership because 'She is not shy of being a girlie... I can respect a woman who has not 'sold out' and become some sort of androgynous super creature.'

Claire comments that, 'if you are a woman in business, be proud of being a woman. It's not going to hold you back, so don't try and be a man. I know a lot of women think that to get up the career ladder they have to behave like a man. They think "that guy up there is successful, he behaves like that, so I need to behave like that to get where he is." Well no you don't. There are many roads to Rome – you don't need to take the same one as everyone else.'

Claire advises women looking to start their own business to do it not because they want to prove a point but because they believe they can make a success of it. However she counsels to only do so having considered the impact on everything else:

In my experience you compromise your family to a degree if you choose to set up and run a business, unless you are running a very small one-man band where it's just you, and you can work when you want, doing what you want. But if you're running a business that employs other people, there will have to be a compromise. You have to be very honest with yourself about whether you're willing to make that compromise and understand what that compromise might be.

Claire speaks from first-hand experience. When she realised that everyone (the company, her partner and her children) apart from herself was getting 'Claire time' she knew she had to be brutally honest about knowing her own limits; she couldn't do it all.

I wasn't being as brilliant an MD as I could be, as brilliant a mum as I could be, as brilliant a wife as I could be. The decision I chose to make – and I was fortunate enough that the business was sufficiently established to do it –

was that when my children were six and eight, I sent them to a weekly boarding school. The company was turning over about £15m with around 45 staff and I just wasn't doing everything very well. I decided I would focus on the business during the week and my children at weekends.

> ## *Advice to other* ENTREPRENEURS
>
> Never compromise when recruiting staff.

Claire has no concerns about the impact on her children, now thriving teenagers of 13 and 15:

They are so fantastically rounded. I have no regrets – not one – because they've grown up to be independent and brilliantly confident kids. It was a compromise but it was one I was prepared to make. Some people wouldn't dream of sending their children away to school, but for me it wasn't going to work any other way.

Claire makes no apologies for admitting she wasn't a 'natural' mother. 'Some people adore spending time in the park, building Lego, making plasticine models and can think of nothing better. I get bored senseless doing that, I was OK admitting that; it doesn't mean I was a bad mother', she says. 'I tried to do what was going to work best for everyone. I was actually quite confident about saying "this is what I'm really good at, this is how I can best use my skills, and the bits I'm not so good at, I can get someone else to do."'

In September 2006, as a reflection of the increased size and breadth of the services the company offered, Stopgap changed its name to The SG Group. This encompassed the original Stopgap for freelance marketing recruitment, RightStop for permanent marketing roles, Fitzroy for senior marketing search and selection, and Courtenay HR (acquired in March 2006) for HR recruitment.

Looking back, Claire says that one of the real benefits of running your own business is doing it your way. 'You determine the rules of the game', she says finally. 'The privilege of owning the business and still being involved is that I can create something that I'm proud of and that I *want* to be involved with. That might not make it the most financially successful business but my rules say that isn't the number one driver. Other people would do something very different but I choose to create a balance between making a profit and making a business that people want to do business with and that has a fantastic reputation.'

pineapple

Debbie Moore

'**My** idea of an exit plan', says Debbie Moore, 'is to drop dead in Studio 1 at the age of 90.'

This is an appropriate riposte from a woman who surely ranks in any entrepreneurial hall of fame. The first woman chairman to take her company public and be admitted to the floor of the Stock Exchange, she is also the woman who runs the world's best-known dance centre and a woman who has made her fortune on a brand named after a prickly tropical fruit.

It could have all been so different – namely if the derelict warehouse Debbie decided to set up in had been used for bananas, rather than pineapples. But then, that would be another story entirely.

Debbie Moore is the founder and chairman of the Pineapple Dance Studios and fashion company. Established in 1979 and operating out of London's Covent Garden, it has 130 staff and 12 stores in the UK, operating in locations including Bluewater, Lakeside, Manchester's Trafford Centre and Watford's Harlequin Centre. The company also operates in Debenhams stores nationally and internationally, and turnover is currently £10m, with net profit at £1m.

A former model (her first assignment was for *Honey Magazine* in New York) and face of Revlon, the pivotal moment that spurred Debbie into action was the closure of her favourite dance centre in Covent Garden, leaving both teachers and students in Central London with nowhere to go. 'I loved the classes, not least because dance had had such a positive impact on my health', says Debbie.

Undeterred, she collected the signatures of over 2,000 dancers and 50 teachers who promised their support and, crucially, attendance, if she was successful in her ambition to open her own dance centre.

'This gave me a lot of inspiration and was very helpful when the time came to approach the bank for a loan. They could see that I had done my homework, and my forecast for the first year turned out to be spot on', she recalls.

Debbie describes how she secured her initial funding; 'I obtained a loan from a local bank and put my house up as security. I passionately wanted to get my business off the ground, and the fear of failure would never have stopped me taking the risk of starting out on my own.'

Debbie's love for dance was the inspiration throughout the whole set-up process.

I was surrounded in class by the most amazing talent in the world – not only the greatest dancers, but rock stars, film stars…the most creative and energetic people. I came to dance on the recommendation of my homeopathic guru when I wanted to lose weight, who told me that it was the best form of exercise – you use every muscle in your body, and it is very uplifting. I saw instinctively that there was an un-missable opportunity to create a business that I was passionate about, and one that there was a need for.

The passion may have been a positive, but Debbie faced serious hurdles in her plans to convert an old pineapple warehouse into a modern dance studio. As she recalls:

Because I had very little money to play with, I effectively became my own building contractor. Dealing with builders, plumbers and plasterers, and keeping track of everyone was only half the work. I had to deal with cowboy builders, fire cladding the entire building at short notice, and being covered in more concrete dust than make-up for six months. There were also the many building regulators who had to be satisfied that the studios would be safe for public use. Even the drains had a thorough inspection, and we faced many potential delays. First, our fire escape failed to arrive because of the steel strike, so I had to find a company who could provide an approved temporary fire escape made out of scaffolding. Then, the day before we were due to open Pineapple, an inspector deemed an internal mezzanine level unsafe. I had no choice but to have it taken down overnight, so that we would be ready to open in the morning.

An advocate of the shoestring budget, the original Pineapple logo was designed by her next-door neighbour, and a lot of Debbie's research was done via the *Yellow Pages.*

Dancers being put through their paces

'I've always put everything back into the business', she says. 'I never got fabulous offices or cars. Offices don't make money so I just had a corner of a room near the studio. It was a big challenge in the beginning.'

The first Pineapple studios opened its doors to the public in 1979. In-keeping with Debbie's philosophy that 'to dance is to live', the centre offered a range of classes aiming to attract people from all walks of life.

'I did make a profit in the first year, which was unusual', she remembers. However, just a few years later, in 1983, Pineapple effectively stopped for Debbie; her daughter Lara, aged 10, was paralysed from a spinal haemorrhage, and she devoted her time to searching for a cure.

Pineapple refused to stand still, and its second studio, Pineapple West in Baker Street, launched in 1981. More studios followed, in New York's Broadway and London's Kensington.

Two years later, with Lara sufficiently recovered for Debbie to return her attention to her business, she focused on expanding the brand into clothing design; which heralded the launch of the iconic Pineapple leg warmers and branded dancewear. To fund the expansion, she realised she needed a huge injection of cash. Debbie took the bold step of floating Pineapple on the stock market and in doing so became the first woman chairman to step onto the trading floor of the London Stock Exchange in November 1982.

'I went public', she says, 'to get the money to expand the business. And you can only go public if you've got three years of doubling your profits, which I managed to do.'

In looking back to that time, Debbie acknowledges her status as one of the founding 'mothers' of women entrepreneurs; 'I was the first woman to take her company public. I think it's quite extraordinary that it took until 1982 to be the first woman. It took a model with a dance studio and a dream to be the first woman. All I did was show what was possible', she says. 'I don't see myself as this clever businesswoman, I just see myself as a role model in the sense that if I can, anyone can.'

In recognition of her achievements as an entrepreneur, Debbie was awarded the Veuve Clicquot Businesswoman of the Year Award in 1984.

However, over the next few years, Debbie grew unhappy with the direction the company was taking. She felt there was too much focus on profit at the expense of its entrepreneurial spirit. 'You can't work with people who only see the money. They're very short-sighted', she says. Therefore, in 1988 she fought to buy her company back. That year also coincided with a further decline in daughter Lara's health, and Pineapple once more took a back seat.

Debbie used the time to write her own book, *When A Woman Means Business*, published in 1989. Containing her own unique blend of business advice and experience, the book offers an insight into her often-challenging personal relationships.

When I started, my husband was absolutely against it. He asked why I couldn't do something small, like his partner's wife, and open a boutique or something. I told him that he was following his own career and he didn't need to get involved, and he said, "well what if it fails, and I'm a high-profile accountant?" So I said, well don't come near it then!

And he didn't until Pineapple was about to go public.

'He then wanted to take the kudos', says Debbie matter-of-factly. 'He didn't take us there. I thought that if he leaves me just because I want to do what I want to do with my life, it doesn't say much for our relationship anyway.'

They later divorced, and she has not remarried. 'I've done my marrying', she says frankly. 'My divorce was all over the papers and I remember saying that as long as they spelt Pineapple right, I didn't care. It's when they stop writing about you that you should worry.'

Debbie admits she wrote the book in response to the many letters she received from women who wanted to start their own businesses, but felt held back by their husband or partner and own lack of confidence.

The main essence of the book was to let women know that you're not born with confidence. You have to be brave, have courage and be prepared to work hard. The confidence comes with just making it happen. I often said to women that if you want to do it, you do it. Whether you work, or you don't work, he's still going to run off with the secretary! He's not going to leave you because you work. He might leave you because you don't work! You have to do what's right for you.

In doing what's right for her business, Debbie knows that it's vital to have a good support staff. 'With a strong team you can climb mountains', she says. 'Any bad apples have to be taken out very quickly, and any politics that are developing, even in small companies, have to be stamped out.'

Some of Debbie's tactics that are more unusual have been hiring staff using astrological charts and graphology (analysing handwriting) to gauge their suitability.

Meanwhile, Pineapple secured its first big licensing deal in 2000. 'We are the leading brand in Debenhams, in children's and ladies wear and we are now launching the product brand globally', says Debbie. 'The move has been a tremendous success, as Debenhams did £50m on our brand last year.'

'You have to be careful who you choose as partners when you are licensing', advises Debbie. 'They can destroy your brand. But I thought what they were doing with the profile of their stores and brand fitted in with us. They're young girls who shop in our shops – no one ever wants anything bigger than a size 12. So in Debenhams, it gave me the opportunity to go up to size 20.'

Debbie still loves what she does but admits its not easy being in the clothing business.

'You are always at the mercy of your suppliers and it's getting more and more difficult because of people like Primark and Hennes; people who command massive quantities. Designing your own and getting it made is much more difficult than it used to be. They always want to have minimums of 1,000 per colour, and the likes of Asda are getting a hundred thousand. It's quite a difficult place to be', she says.

The brand she established over two decades ago is showing no signs of diminishing. 'The studios are still the biggest dance centre in the world', says Debbie. 'It's still the biggest space offering open classes for dancers to come from all walks of life. I still design the clothes, and my office is behind the shop. I'm 25/8 now. They used to call it 24/7. I am very hands on!' she laughs.

She advises other entrepreneurs to keep a tight rein on their purse strings, saying 'there's no such thing as a free lunch. Be prepared to work hard and not start spending the money before you've made it. If you're only doing it to make money then you're already dead.'

Advice to other ENTREPRENEURS

Don't spend your money before you've made it. Be brave, have courage and be prepared to work hard.

Debbie also suggests researching business startup schemes. 'I took advantage of the business-expansion scheme that Margaret Thatcher set up at one point. It was easier for me. I had a woman prime minister at the time so in some way there were more opportunities for women.'

'I've learnt by all my mistakes', says Debbie finally.

You just grow. You make mistakes and wrong decisions but at least it's a decision and you have to remember not to have fear. It's only a job. It's not life and death. That's easy for me to say because of what I've been through with Lara. I come from the north of England and have a work ethic. I feel that I didn't have a great education; I just had energy and courage. I was a model for 18 years, I travelled, I met wonderful people, and then when my career was coming to an end, I wanted to make sure I had something amazing to do because I couldn't imagine after that kind of a job staying at home with the kids, because I'd done so much. I'm fortunate to have such an interesting life but it's been blood, sweat, tears and fire-fighting; hiring and firing and not being able to pay the rent and VAT. It's been a long, hard slog to get to where we are now where we are very successful and the brand is known all over the world.

Admitting that the studios are still her favourite part of the business, Debbie admits that her resolution for the next few months is to dance more; 'perhaps try some flamenco. Or maybe some tango. But definitely', she says, 'some pole dancing.'

———————— *JW* ————————

Dr Glenda Stone

'**Y**ou're a diva of your own destiny and if you want to do something completely different and new then why not?' asks Glenda Stone.

The founder and CEO of Aurora, a London city-based company that provides the highly successful wheretowork.com company-comparison jobsite and marketing services to over 100 blue-chip clients globally, has come a long way since teaching in the Australian outback.

Over the years Glenda has gained a vast amount of experience, from manager to entrepreneur, from government policy maker to business angel.

Married with a young son, Glenda has always been attracted by entrepreneurial vision so running her own show was a natural progression. Glenda's mental light bulb clicked when she discovered an untapped opportunity in the UK; 'business and professional women had not been specifically targeted as a market to be recruited or sold to', she explains.

The burst of inspiration happened to coincide with an unplanned shift in her personal circumstances: meeting her future husband abroad whilst travelling on a break from work. She admits that her 'world changed because it was a whirlwind romance and we married within five months of meeting.'

I moved continents and knew that I had three choices. Either I could work for the UK government (as government had been my background), I could work for a corporate – but at that time I thought 'well which one's better and which one has the most opportunities?' (and there wasn't much information around), or I could start a company and finally satisfy my entrepreneurial drive.

Glenda spent 12 months in the UK working in international trade and investment and doing lots of technology courses before she came up with the idea for Aurora, which she launched in 2000.

Her previous experience in Australia was key in shaping the concept. As assistant executive director in the Women's Unit in the Queensland Treasury, her focus had been on gender from a business and work perspective. 'I quickly understood that blue-chip companies desperately wanted to recruit and/or sell to the women's market', she says. 'Thus, I developed Aurora as a trusted and reliable channel into that market.'

Aurora firstly began as a women's network with high-profile business events and Glenda was confident that both the corporates and the women found these of huge value:

Women were getting something satisfying, rewarding and useful out of the events while Aurora, as a business, was generating revenue from the events because we were getting paid to be that channel to market. The corporates were also getting something out of it because they were being marketed in very targeted and discerning ways and were seeing great outputs.

Glenda did her homework, researching the market and her potential competitors.

I was quite diligent and it was very extensive. There weren't many social networks around at that time; the only kind of women's networks back then

Aurora runs the successful wheretowork.com company comparison jobsite

were the traditional ones, but they all had more of a social agenda rather than a business agenda. My agenda was focusing more on business growth and career growth rather than the social networking side.

Glenda initially invested £20,000 of her own money on starting a web design company in the six months prior to Aurora. This was to enable her to learn more about technology and building websites and CRM databases.

'I bought my first company assets with that money', she recalls, 'and then to further fund the business I developed websites for clients – about 30 websites in that time. At that point I had the skills to start developing our own site for Aurora. It was kind of like a practical MBA with the tech component; learning about business and doing VAT returns. Clearly Aurora as a business has moved on and our website is obviously far more sophisticated than my first attempts!'

So at the very beginning of Aurora, revenue was derived solely from event management. As Glenda recalls:

Our revenue came from women buying tickets for our business events and from corporate sponsors. The margins aren't fantastic because it's money in, money out – you've got a lot of overheads and expenses. However, while we were delivering these great events for the blue-chip market we were also developing our community – our network.

With their first Aurora event in July 2000, the next couple of years saw a swift progression to two major corporate and entrepreneurial events each month. 'Some years we ran 75 events per annum. It really was a huge amount', says Glenda.

For that first crucial year of growing the business, Glenda pretty much did it all; 'it was me and my pink fluffy slippers at home doing everything from the massive mail outs to building the website, sales, making the name badges and chairing the events. It was absolutely everything.'

Her work paid off as companies quickly became interested in Aurora because of its access and insight into the female demographic: their needs, how they buy, what they buy, and where they want to work.

'We became recognised as an expert company in terms of organisations that wanted to focus on business and working women', says Glenda, 'therefore we started to do quite a bit of consultancy on how to recruit, retain and develop women. We were also advising companies on how to position business products and services to women. Unfortunately everyone wanted me, they didn't want my staff. I thought "this is crazy; we'll never scale up the business if I don't do something to remove myself from it." So that's when we thought, right, let's put all the consulting tools and ideas and processes in software, and that's what we did!'

Following a successful pilot in 2002 with 12 blue-chip companies, Aurora subsequently launched wherewomenwanttowork.com in 2003 and started selling licenses furiously. Glenda knew exactly the companies she wanted to firstly get on board and actively sought them out. The highly successful company comparison jobsite has now become, simply, wheretowork.com and is used by corporate clients in over 17 different countries to recruit top talent. The jobsite is powered by Aurora's bespoke software that provides a range of market intelligence tools and data on the back-end of the site.

'Once you've got one corporate client, the second one's easier, the third one's easier, the fourth one's easier...you get that snowball effect', she says.

Through the site, users can research and compare companies based on their needs and interests as well as apply for relevant jobs. Companies enjoy this highly effective channel for marketing their employer brand to discerning candidates.

Aurora was initially called 'Busygirl' but by 2002 Glenda wasn't comfortable that this name sat well with the blue-chip clients.

We needed a more grown up name, so we re-branded to 'Aurora'. Aurora means 'goddess of the dawn' and that's very relevant to our company because we always spot the first snippets of change and what's new on the horizon. We're always pushing the edges; we're always innovating and leading the market in what we do. The dawn is all about new ideas.

The structure of the business means Aurora has, according to Glenda, never had any issues regarding lack of finance. 'We've always been a cash-rich company because, for example, our jobsite revenue comes from an upfront annual licence payment from each corporate client. That's very different from a business in retail with consumer products where you're having to buy stock, hold it, sell it on, and you're working on smaller margins.'

Role MODEL

I don't have one specific mentor, as my 'mentor model' requires a flexible group of business-savvy people who are my sounding boards and inspiration. But if there was one person I'd love to have an hour of time with it would absolutely have to be Rupert Murdoch.

The range of projects Aurora has worked on is impressive and ranges from women-focused marketing for blue-chip organizations to 'the Blackberry Women and Technology Awards' for Blackberry, women's business events for HSBC and women's technology events for BT. More currently, Aurora has worked on employer branding projects for global companies. The Aurora Women's Network itself now has a membership in excess of 28,000 members and is a unique and highly targeted channel to market.

Glenda has found that people, product and processes are key to success in the first years of any business. She also strongly advocates being careful with your money:

You can't cut corners; you've got to have a robust and scaleable, reliable, approach because with corporate software development it has got to work and it can't have any risk attached. So yes, you've got to pay oodles for your hosting, oodles for your software, oodles for your hardware, oodles for good people – because at the end of the day you get what you pay for if you're lucky.

With so much invested in its technology, Glenda is unequivocal when it comes to protecting Aurora's systems. 'Security is a huge issue. Our corporate clients' reputations are at stake', says Glenda. 'It's just constant because the more you grow, the more your needs grow. The more the expense grows, the more the risk grows. For us, we have very tight contracts with all our corporate clients because we're managing their reputation online, through our site. There are certain standards and levels that we must maintain and we must constantly review, monitor and meet.'

Glenda's business plan for Aurora has naturally changed over time, from being 'quite a thick document to quite a thin, focused, succinct, pragmatic document. Again, you're constantly revising, refocusing. There is that saying "failing to plan is planning to fail" and I do honestly believe that, because you need focus and you need strategy, you need measurement of outputs.'

One of the constant focuses for Aurora is meeting client expectations.

You have to be low-risk to them, so you have to look the piece, you have to have the right processes and you have to have the right mindset. You have to have a very close understanding of their needs, their culture and their reputations and you must ensure that you never do anything to compromise that.

When it comes to number crunching, Glenda is very much focused on diligence and her mantra is 'efficiency, efficiency, efficiency'.

'It just breaks our hearts to see any money wasted. We're turning over great revenue on good margins but you're always still looking for vertical markets to keep up-selling', she says.

> ## Advice to other
> # ENTREPRENEURS
>
> Focus very specifically; smaller at first but do it well and grow from there. You can always do the other things later when you're bigger and you have more resources.

Whilst she admits she spends more time focused on her work rather than her home life, Glenda still says she enjoys it.

> *I don't like to work on a balance because balance implies 50:50 and if you talk to most entrepreneurs they are most relaxed when they're working. They love working; they're driven. It's something they created and are running and doing so I'd much rather be doing that than watching TV or doing the housework. The stuff I don't have time for I outsource – I have cleaners and other support around me. I do like downtime, don't get me wrong, and reading books in the bath is very nice, I just don't get to do it that often.*

As for reconciling being a mother and a businesswoman, Glenda says she finds ways to make it work for her.

> *You've got to make the decision between being with your child or being at some meeting you don't really see the point of. My son is only a few months old and I'm thinking "do I need a nanny? Do I need to put him in nursery? Do I need to stay home with him? Do I need to bring him to the office?" and I do a combination of all those things. So, for example, I've got my son in the office with me today, I managed to get to the hairdressers this morning and I've had a few meetings, I've done those by teleconference rather than going out to the client. When you're working in a corporate you've got maternity leave and you're 'on' or you're 'off' whereas what I see with women entrepreneurs is that ability to morph those spheres of your life in a more seamless way.*

Aurora has now expanded from a one-woman band to eight full-time and six part-time staff but Glenda is still very hands on with the business. 'You still find yourself doing many broad different things', she explains. 'My sole responsibility now is managing new and existing business, so on any given day I will be talking to maybe 12–15 corporate clients alongside our client services team.'

Still, the workload has reaped some prestigious rewards. Glenda won a Business Vision Award in 2004, was awarded Pioneer of the Nation by HM the Queen in 2003, and won European Businesswoman of the Year in 2002. In 2004 she received an honorary doctorate from Leeds Metropolitan University and in 2006 was appointed co-chair of Gordon Brown's Women's Enterprise Taskforce that aims to increase the quantity and scalability of women's enterprise in the UK. In 2007 Glenda was recognised by HRH The Queen as one of the Top 200 Women in Business in Britain.

As for the future, Glenda is open to new ideas but knows it would be in a brand new sector, 'something in renewable energy, property or finance. I'm good at structure, process, operations and sales – and I love transferring that to technology', she says.

It's clear, however, that whatever project she's working on or sector she's in, Glenda loves being her own boss.

You have the freedom to create, develop, grow and achieve. I love waking up every morning and thinking 'I can make as much money as I can today.' Whereas if you're in a corporate you're going to earn your £250 a day or whatever the hell you earn. Being an entrepreneur you've got this un-boundaried opportunity which is nice, it's like clear blue sky.

L♥ve Those Sh♥es

Glenys Berd

If you need any convincing that shoes can be good for your health, meet Glenys (Glen) Berd, founder of online shoe specialist www.lovethoseshoes.com.

Ranked 30th in the Top Entrepreneurs in Britain list, Glen is no stranger to enterprise. She set up her first business with her then-boyfriend on leaving college. They married, and their soft furnishings store gradually grew into a larger interior design venture, specialising in show homes. However, the relationship didn't last; they divorced and she took over the business.

Fascinated by the internet and its possibilities, Glen met her business partner, former Cable & Wireless employee, Nick Evans. With her enthusiasm and his tech-savvy approach, together they set up online fashion business, LadyBwear.com in 1998, providing women's 'fantasy' clothes in sizes six to 36.

'He had an idea that business on the internet was possible', recalls Glen. 'It wasn't being done then because the internet was mainly being used by large companies who had vanity sites, notice boards and news groups. I was really looking for something new so we just talked it all out. I don't know when that first spark came that said "let's start a business", but it was just one of those things. In the beginning, it was "how can I put my interior design company on the internet?" It kind of grew from that.'

The concept for LadyBwear came about by accident rather than design. One of her machinists from the original interiors business had been a tailor in Bosnia, and together they started designing 'simple garments' and began selling them online.

With the internet still very raw, Glen says it was then very challenging to promote her fledgling business:

There were very few websites in those days – we'd perhaps go on shopping directories, but it was awfully difficult. You couldn't do UK pounds transactions anywhere on the internet. Everything was in US dollars. There were no companies that would take credit cards or anything. We started off doing sizes UK 6 to UK 36, so we discovered this niche market; there were lots and lots of very tiny people and lots of very large people who couldn't buy 'with it' clothes. We played on the 'made in Britain' thing; the Americans loved anything that was British.

Glen likens those early days to the Wild West; 'people that were buying were learning; people that were selling were learning; we were all learning the internet at the same time. It was real kind of cowboy country, if you know what I mean. I don't mean "cowboys", but it was just so *green*, nobody knew what they were doing.'

Glen established the business without any outside funding stating that 'all the finance (£5,000) was from our own resources.' She was able to take a salary after just 18 months.

'We survived the dot-com bubble burst without any help. Through hard work, persistence, good ideas and being single-minded, we have proved anyone can do it without venture capital and the like.'

By 2003 Glen was impatient for another business 'buzz', something to stretch and challenge her. Whilst on the lookout for a new pair of trainers, she came across MBT: Masai Barefoot Technology.

Best foot forward: Glen with some of her shoe range

'I was in a waiting room somewhere', she recalls, 'and there was a really old, dog-eared magazine with a little article in it about a Swiss scientist who had made this shoe. He had been a footballer and put some technology into it. It was a tiny little five-line article, I don't know what made me cut it out.'

The medical shoes were only then available in Switzerland and Austria. Glen got in touch and offered to sell them online. 'He laughed, and said "don't be silly, you can't sell shoes over the internet, you have to try shoes on, and anyway, there aren't any here yet!"' she recalls.

Not one to be put off, Glen arranged a meeting. 'He was an ex-business consultant and was thinking about bringing these shoes here to work in clinics and yoga practices. We left that meeting with the idea and said "OK, we'll set up a website for you and one for us, and we'll sell the shoes", and that's what we did.'

Three weeks after the meeting, the website was up and running. They were selling around three pairs a week for the first two months. Then an article in *The Sunday Times Style* magazine changed everything by describing them in a manner many women would find appealing. They used the magic words "cellulite busters". 'And the whole world exploded – it went mad!' recalls Glen.

Demand was huge with thousands of customers waiting for their orders to be shipped. 'We just had to keep saying "sorry, they're on the sea." In fact, I wrote a daily diary about where the shoes were, what was happening and what the situation was, so people used to log on every day and read this daily diary about what was going on. It created a community of people waiting for their shoes!'

Putting her best foot forward, Glen continued to look for some more innovative footwear and came across the Earth shoes with their 'amazing technology of negative heels which improve posture and circulation, tone muscles, reduce cellulite, ease and even cure back pain.'

Following her instinct and impulse, Glen sourced some samples and began selling them online. In 2005, Love Those Shoes signed a contract with Earth worth £30m over the next five years, for exclusive distribution in the UK and Europe. Glen had discovered a niche market for 'healthy' footwear.

If you're going to walk and wear shoes, you may as well wear ones that do you good. I actively looked for other shoes that do the same thing. What I look for is something that's not already here, that is brand new; a new technology.

We take things on which are actually quite green and we nurture them, we promote them, and we do the PR on them.

Glen started in her design studio with the boxes of shoes mixed in with her sewing machines and clothes stock. Swiftly outgrowing her interior design studio, they moved to larger premises, and then extended into the premises next door as well. With 10 staff, the company now works out of an office in Stockport, near Manchester, but trades globally via the internet.

Current footwear on lovethoseshoes.com includes the zero-carbon-footprint shoe, crocs, and a totally organic hempathy range. Ethically aware clients include actress Gwyneth Paltrow.

As the market was an untapped one, Glen says there wasn't much they could do in the way of preparatory market research. She says 'it was basically a belief in the idea working, rather than doing research to obtain proof that it would. We learned what to do by listening very closely to the customers, and then constantly adjusting the business according to what we learned from that.'

She did prepare a business plan, but admits that it changes regularly; 'it's more of a direction that's applicable today, but may not be tomorrow.'

Ever forthright in her opinions, Glen says that going to a bank for business support would have been a waste of time for her. 'They're rubbish at business and their advice would be worthless. We work on an overdraft basis supported with guarantees. Maybe when we are a multi-*multi*-millionaire business and they're knocking on our door there may be someone with more knowledge put on our case. But by then we won't need them either.'

Role MODEL

My main mentor is my mother, who has been a brilliant businesswoman all her life, and gave me the background and environment to follow in her footsteps. She is an amazing fighter and has taught me that anything is possible if you put your mind to it and never give up. As for one I would like to meet – that would be a toss up between Richard Branson and Alan Sugar. They have both done rather well in business!

To date, turnover is around £1.8m. However, Glen is coy when it comes to revealing anything further: 'we are in profit but it's commercially sensitive – or everyone will want to do it!'

Glen doesn't believe in outsourcing – she likes to do everything herself.

Talk about learning lessons – we outsourced to a fulfilment house. It was a total nightmare. The mistakes they made…they duplicated orders, we had customer service nightmares afterwards, and it was just terrible dealing with them. I suppose they're only as good as their staff, but they made a lot of mistakes as well. So we brought it all back in house.

But Glen admits she wouldn't be where she is today if the mistakes hadn't propelled the business on faster. She bemoans the difficulties in getting the right staff through the door and says average candidates looking for an easy nine to five need not apply:

We are a very different company to work for. If they've been in a corporate environment and then they come to a small business, all of a sudden, they've got to think more. We treat all our staff as adults; there aren't manuals for them to be guided by. Lots of people can't handle that as well. The fact that you're working in a small team of 10 or 12 people – you have to know everything that's going on, you have to be aware that somebody else has to pick up if you drop, or if somebody's off sick someone else has to step in – everybody has to multi-task.

She's proud that every member of her team is committed to growing the business:

They want it to grow, they want to grow with it, they're excited by the buzz and we are very fast working. We'll suddenly find a new brand and want to get it to market really fast – we could probably turn it round within two or three weeks – so we get it on the website, get the deal set up, get press releases out and articles in, and then the phones will go mad. Everybody jumps on the phones, then the container arrives so everybody's down in the warehouse.

Love Those Shoes is presented with around 500 different shoe styles ahead of each season. They then select the range they will run across Europe.

That's what women want, to look stylish while it's doing them good; their secret friend on their feet. I don't want the things to look like orthopaedic shoes – it's a fashion item and it's about technology being put into what people wear

Advice to other ENTREPRENEURS

Have self belief and trust your instincts.

today. Our biggest sellers are trainers and sports shoes – they're so popular and fashionable now. I like to think I select them with fashion in mind as well!

Marketing is very much a team effort but Glen admits she has to be involved with absolutely every part of the business. 'You've always got to have an overview', she says, 'and a hands-on management for running it – not because people can't make decisions, but you've got to plan the direction of the business, where you want to go. Only you see where you want to be in a year's time or five years' time.'

The business is continually expanding and Love Those Shoes has just taken on a completely new brand, the Power Diet Weight Technology Shoes whose interchangeable weighted insoles burn an extra 300 calories in 30 minutes. Glen is also busy sourcing specific 'fabulous' products for people with arthritis and diabetes.

She promotes the business via online search engines and a weekly email newsletter and offline via PR, but news of the business is mainly spread though word of mouth.

Never quite sure where her bursts of business inspiration come from, Glen says the ideas 'just come from my head and I don't know how or why.' She says her proudest achievement is growing a business from scratch in a market she knew nothing about, selling an unknown product using technology she didn't understand and with no funding.

Not one to rest easily on her laurels, Glen is also working on her latest venture, a digital photo-frame business, lovethosepictures.com. She's also made the difficult decision of gradually closing down LadyBwear as Love Those Shoes eats up more of her energy and resources.

To be successful, Glen believes you have to be single-minded and persistent, and to believe in yourself. 'You've got to believe what you think is right so go with your gut instinct', she says.

Invariably, it is right and it will work out. If it doesn't, then you've learned what you can do yourself. I think the hesitation in most people is what would stop them doing things – you can't. You've just got to go for it. Running my own business means I can make my own decisions. This is ultimate freedom for me. I make my own mistakes, but also make my own benefits. The restrictive aspect is I can never leave it, the responsibility never goes away.

———— *JW* ————

JCPR

Jackie Cooper

'**B**eing an entrepreneur is a mindset. Either your mind works in that way and you will see fresh opportunities and fresh territory to be exploited or you won't. That's definitely how I work and it's still what excites me. When that stops, you'll have to put me out to pasture.'

So says 45-year-old Jackie Cooper, co-founder of Jackie Cooper PR (JCPR), the public relations agency behind some of the most memorable consumer campaigns of the last two decades, including Wonderbra and PlayStation.

JCPR celebrated its 20th anniversary in 2007, together with a fee income turnover of £6m plus, profit of just under half a million and a staff of 72. And let's not forget major clients such as Mars, Shell and Motorola. Not bad for someone who admits that PR was something she fell into by mistake rather than design.

'None of this was particularly strategic or decisive which probably doesn't sound very impressive but it was something that grew on me', she says.

Jackie's father, himself an entrepreneur, was a huge influence and suggested that PR was the right fit for his daughter, who says she was never academically strong. The seeds of JCPR grew from a career mistake which also reinforced her opinion that 'although money was important to me it wasn't the be-all and end-all of what I was doing.' Realising six weeks into a new job for a 'dreadful PR agency which massaged the client rather than delivered', she happened upon news of an innovative partnership between Greenpeace and edgy 1980's advertising agency, Yellowhammer.

Intrigued by the pairing, she impulsively called the environmental group, and ended up working there for £45 a week.

I did decide that it wasn't PR that I hated but the way PR had been done. I started to love the job again being at Greenpeace; I launched the Anti-Fur Trade campaign which was a seminal campaign of its time and realised that this was still magic. I loved the potential that was achievable with reaching consumers and portraying messaging partly through media, and got a tremendous buzz out of it.

Calls from clients from her former agency led to further freelance projects. Jackie Cooper PR was a natural progression 'born out of discovering that I liked to do the job and didn't really want to get back into the situation where my freedom was curtailed. And freedom of choice has been of huge importance to me ever since.'

Jackie had literally been working off her dining room table before renting an office in Bond Street from PR legend Max Clifford (a turn of events which she laughingly refers to as 'very bizarre.') The business was growing and she was making money.

A copy job for a magazine required an interview with an expert on bridal wear, and portentously she was advised to meet with Robert Phillips, whose route to his own circumstances was as bizarre as her own.

'He was a class academic at university; his father ran an agency selling Italian bridal wear and died very suddenly. Being an Italian company, these guys descended upon his doorstep and said "you are the son of your father, you will carry on." Being Robert and always one for an opportunity, he said "ok." And unknown to them, he was managing to continue to study at university whilst trying to market this bridal wear company', she says.

The current JCPR offices in London's West End

Following their meeting, Robert informed Jackie with utter candour that they were destined to work together for the rest of their lives.

'I thought he was completely nuts and said "lovely to see you, do give me a call if anything comes up", which of course is the great PR line to exit all awkward situations', she recalls. However, Robert did call the next day, with an opportunity to pitch together for the then-giant of the British high street, Sears. Fast forward and the two found themselves on a train making a pitch for the huge retail business and ultimately walking away with their first joint piece of business, 'without a business card between us.'

Still protective of her freedom, the two worked together for a year on various projects whilst still running their own businesses. 'But', says Jackie, 'after a year it seemed to make sense to join up. We believed that we could really make a difference and that there was so much more to be done with PR than was being done by any of our competitors. We wanted to do class work, simplify the way it was being delivered and trail blaze where we were going. And that's how he became my partner.'

Whilst Jackie admits Robert had more of a natural affinity for numbers, at the beginning their roles were evenly split. They both ran campaigns, both spoke to clients, and both came up with the creative delivery for their client base.

It wasn't all plain sailing, and as Jackie says frankly, 'these things are never fairytale stories. I knew how to do PR and this was his first 'proper' job out of university. We had lots of vim and vigour and a huge amount of belief but what is underestimated when you start your own business is that you have to be skilled at two things: the thing that you are offering as your business offer and at actually running the business. Neither of us were particularly skilled at running a business. We were incredibly naïve.'

It was that inexperience which led to several 'ridiculous mistakes' very early on. Their first office contents were almost entirely leased, which Jackie describes as being 'just the most ridiculous way of going forward' as they were effectively overpaying for office kit.

'We just didn't understand the fundamentals about running a business', she says. 'You need to have a business plan that's bedded down in business skill and a service skill. You have to get more dough coming in than you have got going out. That sounds utterly obvious now but we just didn't have enough of an overview on it – we just assumed that because we had a good client base and because we were turning over good money, that it would all come to be.'

Their first accountant was, by her own admission, terrible. They ended up cap in hand at the bank, admitting they had a problem and had over-extended themselves, and needed their support whilst they traded out of a £100,000 debt.

'We had no capital and no funding at the beginning. We had no investment and we actually started with a debt pretty early on and set ourselves a target that we not only break even but break a profit, without getting any funding at all. And that's what we did.'

They received an incredible amount of support from the people around them, even in the most unlikely quarters, including the 'guardian angel' of a bank manager based in Moorgate ('it was actually my father's bank, otherwise they probably would have arrested us on the spot!'). Her father was one of her staunchest allies, paying their salary bill during the months when they could not afford to.

Role MODEL

The biggest inspiration in my life was my Dad. He was an entrepreneur all his life. His trailblazing business initiative matched with his 'never give up' attitude was a real lesson to me. He was a courteous gentleman, but he also had a wicked black sense of humour which, thankfully, I have inherited.

I have been blessed with many relationships in my life that have supported, motivated and inspired me. These include the constant and unwavering presence of my pragmatic and ever-loving, long-suffering, wise husband David; the 20-year partnership I have enjoyed with my co-founder and co-partner in crime, Robert Phillips, and the solid faith of one of my earliest clients – a guy called John Rowley – who had such belief in my ability that led to the formation of JCPR originally. Without him there would not have been a JCPR and without him I would not have learned how to effectively manage the stresses and strains of clients, banks and staff while still reaching for your dream.

It was very much hand to mouth and incredibly scary, but you learn a lot of very tough business lessons when you're put in that position and it makes you much more fine-tuned to being smarter going forward. The business plan was very much driven by the bank who asked if we had one. And we suddenly thought, 'oh shit, no we haven't!' We had to do it from a defensive position which is the worst place to do a business plan from; having to go to the bank and make them understand that we had enough insight and vision to assure them that this was a viable business.

Whilst their passion and zeal ensured they had no problem attracting new staff to the business, they soon realised that it wasn't just their own professional lives they were gambling with;

Putting my own financial future on the line is one thing; other people's financial future on the line was another. Robert and I took that very seriously. We thought, 'bloody hell, we're responsible for the well-being of these people, we really ought to know what we're doing because they're relying on us for their rent and their food.'

For the first few years, Jackie and Robert poured everything back into the business. Their innovative campaigns formed the backbone of their marketing efforts. They moved offices twice before settling at their current home in the West End's New Cavendish Street.

Our new business drive has very much been fuelled by people seeing our work, liking the campaigns that we deliver and coming to us. We had and we still do have a very clear view of who we were pitching against, what their offer was and why we were different. That was supported by the fact that when we won business, the feedback we got was that 'we employed you because you were so different.'

When considering if there has ever been a point when she's realised she's 'made it', Jackie is thoughtful: 'that', she says, 'is a conversation we've probably had a hundred times over the last 20 years; when we paid the bank off and didn't owe them anything and got our guarantees back we asked "have we made it?" Each time we moved into a new building we asked "have we made it?" When we sold the company to Edelman, it didn't really seem like it then, and when Robert was made CEO of the Edelman Group of Companies and I was made vice chair and creative director, it still hasn't felt like we've made it. I think there's something about the need for progress that drives us still, God knows why, but that means we can never really feel we can put a stake in the ground and say "that's it.'"

For someone who has made their living promoting brands in the global media arena, Jackie surprisingly admits to being shy. Although she says that, she is quite different when it comes to talking about brands or the work that they do:

> *Advice to other*
> # ENTREPRENEURS
>
> Be passionate about what you're doing, speak to as many people as you can and surround yourself with people who are great at the things you find difficult.

The passion takes over. I look at some of the people who've promoted themselves really well, in terms of really using their personality to get their brand story across and I don't think that's something that I've done because I've not been comfortable in the past doing it. I am more comfortable doing it now, but its not the way we've built the business or built the profile of the agency.

She advises anyone looking to start their own business to be prepared for the manifold challenges it presents:

You've got to make it happen for you in an area that you love and know. You have to have the conviction and the desire. If you are not astute at running a business yourself, make sure you have somebody in the business or as a consultant to give you that advice. I'd also recommend my dad's advice: 'speak to everybody' because you never know who leads to what, and what that can trigger.

She also advises against trying to be something you are not:

I love being a woman in business. I'm not one of these women who tries to be a man; I think it's quite exhausting if you think you have to fight sex battles or demographic battles. I'm not a university graduate. I am what I am and I can only be what I can be and I think you have to take control of what you can do and not feel bad about the stuff you can't do. There are far more things that I can't do than I can. But I've been very lucky and probably quite smart in being able to say 'I'm good at this, but I'm absolutely shit at all of the other things so I need to make sure I surround myself with people who are great at things I'm not good at.'

By the time she'd had her eldest daughter at 33, Jackie had broken the back of building the business. She doesn't think she could have done it any other way.

I pointedly haven't taken part in any articles that are headlined 'women who have it all' because I think that's complete bullshit. I don't think women can have it all. I think I probably muck something up every day whether it's at home or at work. I have no idea whether I am doing this work–life-balance thing well. If both my kids end up in therapy, you'll know that I've screwed up! It's a battle and I see women battling all the time. On the other hand, I look at my daughters and they see me work and I think it's a good thing. There is nothing wrong with a work ethic.

In 2004, Jackie and Robert sold the business to Daniel J Edelman, the world's largest independent PR firm. The two companies formally merged in April 2007. Whilst clearly a successful move for Jackie, she insists establishing JCPR was never the route to riches.

I'm very well off. I don't mean financially, I mean lucky in where we got to from a start of a £100,000 bank debt to being worth anything at all. But we continue to work. If I knew then what I know now, we'd have had a much easier life in terms of enjoying the work more rather than being driven by fear of failure – which we were too much in the early days.

With Edelman's backing and on the understanding that she still needs to be entrepreneurial, she is setting up a separate business offer, providing consultative advice between India and the rest of the world.

With all she has accomplished professionally, Jackie is still most proud of her marriage and two daughters, Megan and Zara. 'The home thing gives me the bedrock to go in and fight and then go home and be re-charged. Without them, I am not sure I would be able to continue to drive it with the passion that I have.'

JANE PACKER

LONDON

Jane Packer

'**I am quite fickle with** my favourite flowers', says international florist Jane Packer, 'but I love peonies – you know those big blousy flowers.'

Jane Packer Flowers launched at a time when being a florist didn't have its current fashionable cachet:

In the early days it was me going to market because there were very few of us in the company; it was me staying late, it was me working Saturdays and Sundays. I literally did work seven days a week for a very long time, but my day now is more about the running of the business and what's next and what we should be doing.

Jane's interest in flowers stemmed from humble beginnings: a Saturday job at her local florist in Essex. She quit school at 17 and moved to London to explore her passion. She worked in other flower shops, went to college and did a City and Guilds floristry course for a few years.

Getting a job as in-house florist to a hotel in Charing Cross, Jane was told by the manager that if she ever decided to set up on her own, she would have his support. Three months after leaving the hotel, Jane returned, realising this was too good an offer to miss.

I was very young, only just 21, and very naïve to start. I knew nothing about business at all, I just thought it could be fun. I learned on the job and did make mistakes. I didn't have any money so I couldn't afford to print out glossy brochures or anything like that – I just sent people some flowers to land on their desk. Fortunately, they responded to that. I think things like that can be great to introduce yourself.

Jane Packer established herself in 1982 with a small shop in London's West End. She wanted to be as far removed from the likes of traditional florists as possible, whose style she saw as very formal and structured; 'that's what distinguishes us immediately', says Jane. 'Everything – the ideas and the design – is individual. I think that's the most important thing.'

Whilst popular legend suggests that her business 'breakout' moment was in 1986 when Sarah Ferguson chose Jane Packer to design the flowers for her wedding to Prince Andrew, the impact for Jane was slightly different.

I suppose it probably was my big break, although not financially. People started referring to us as the 'society florist' and we weren't. We have never been that. I wasn't born on the right side of the tracks to be! There was then a danger that people were going to think we were too expensive, and because of that, we certainly weren't overrun with customers.

Jane recalls journalists from all over the world camping outside their tiny shop in James Street:

We had all these press people knocking on the door and I was so frightened that I'd say something incorrectly and they'd run a story. At the time, it was front-page news and it was all about 'what would she wear and what colour would the bridesmaids wear?' It was this huge thing to be involved in.

Jane readily admits they never had a 'grand plan' for the business. 'Quite often I've just relied on opportunities as they've come my way. The telephone rings and someone wants to meet up and has a fantastic idea and off we go', she says.

A Jane Packer floral creation

> *When I first opened my shop, that was it. My ambition was just to pay the rent and keep the shop open. Obviously as you progress, your ambitions grow but I never dreamt that flowers would become as big as they are. I never dreamt I'd be flying off to Korea to create a wedding for someone.*

The business has bloomed since those early days, but Jane admits her rookie error was being too trusting. She recommends ensuring having contracts with clients to provide a safety net for your business.

You do have bad years when people don't pay you thousands and thousands of pounds and suddenly you are in a situation where the bank is knocking on your door. I've been there and managed, touch wood, to survive. But that's what happens when you're a small company; those shits do do those things to you. They know that they're folding but they will still have their orders of hundreds of pounds a week. Don't put all your eggs in one basket. Make sure you are expanding your business and not relying on one customer.

Jane describes the lack of proper maternity leave as being one of the hardest things about working for yourself. She was back to work three weeks after her son, Rebby's, Caesarean birth (she also has a daughter, Lola).

I didn't go back because I wanted to do it, but because it was a case of having to. One of my biggest regrets was not being able to stay home with my children. I used to cry on the street corner every morning because I didn't want to leave them. But what do you do? You have built up this business and that's how you're earning your money. You can't just throw in the towel.

She says dealing with employees properly is another difficult lesson to learn. 'For you, the business is an integral part of your life but for staff, it's not. They don't worry about the problems you may have going on at that time.'

Jane is keen to dispel the myth of floristry being a relaxing profession. 'That's the last thing it is!' she says. 'If you've just been to market and spent between £300 and £500 on flowers, it's not relaxing if you don't sell them! That whole worry of buying too much or not enough can be difficult.'

Her husband and business partner Gary looks after the finance side of things. 'I am involved in the decisions', she says firmly. 'He will give me the pros and cons and we will make the decision together. We work together very well. Some people always say "oh, how's that?" but as far as I'm concerned, it's great.'

One of those key decisions was the launch of the Jane Packer Delivered range. She relishes the consistency it provides. 'That way', says Jane, 'we can control everything from the way it looks to the quality of the flowers. This is where big relay services fall down I think; you ring up to order some flowers in one county and what you get in another county is completely different. And all because the owner of that shop's interpretation of the picture is different to the one you've been shown in the shop where you ordered the flowers.'

Jane is proud that they were one of the first to offer floristry courses specifically through the Jane Packer Flower School, which has been running for around 18 years.

> ## *Role* MODEL
>
> Margaret Howell and Betty Jackson.

From the moment we started, we decided to be really dedicated to the classes. Others who have tapped into the idea have been irresponsible in terms of what they say they're going to teach and actually having enough people on the course. If you're laying out a course and saying this is what we're going to do, then that's what you do.

On hearing that a recent Flower School graduate has won an award for entrepreneurialism, Jane is genuinely pleased. 'That's fantastic to hear', she says. 'The people that we have coming on the courses are incredible. Some of them are lawyers that just feel burnt out or they were high-flying TV producers. I stand in awe of those people. I think to myself, what do you want to be getting up at five in the morning and doing this for? This is stressful too!'

From the early days when Jane Packer was one of the very few florists in London, she now thinks the capital is almost overrun with them:

You stop at the traffic lights and you can almost guarantee that there will be at least one florist there. You could say I'm contributing to that with the Jane Packer Flower School and that's one of the downsides – sending them out with the knowledge. It is tricky from that point of view as there are more and more people entering into the industry – and there are some good people. Now, I am up against the very people that I've taught!

Jane suffered an illness a few years ago and was off work for about a year. During that time, she learnt a valuable lesson: that the business could survive without her. 'It probably did me a bit of a favour. I could step away and be involved in other things that would progress the business rather than just be involved in the day-to-day toil', she says.

Jane's role is now strategic. During the week of our interview she had been working on designs for their 1-800-flowers.com range in the US while the week before that she was working on the Jane Packer candle accessory range for Debenhams. She is also heavily involved in feeding through a steady stream of ideas to the stores in Japan, Korea, New York and Kuwait and says 'we're a lot like a fashion house now – we create spring, summer and autumn/winter projections of ideas.'

Jane retains a down-to-earth approach and makes a point of knowing what's happening and what's going out. She believes there is a skill in knowing what your customer wants and reacts to and stamping your own mark on your product; 'there are times the flowers are presented to me first and I'll say it's not 'Jane Packer'.'

The Jane Packer brand has an element of simplicity. Jane herself doesn't like things 'with a hundred different varieties of flowers in it', preferring instead things to be quite monochromatic:

> *If it's going to be purple, I like it to be shades of purple, rather than purple, pink and white, with everything in it. I do go through certain phases of flowers where some will be very fashionable and wonderful and then we move on. I've never been a great fan of tropical flowers, like some of my competitors.*

She may be a big name with the celebrities, but Jane doesn't always come down to personally attend to any big name that may walk into the store. 'I might be involved in it if it's a meeting or I'm putting the ideas together for them but there are other people in my team now who can do it equally. That's the important thing to remember when building your business – trust.'

The company has the majority of their stock delivered direct from Holland.

> *It means we are able to access flowers from other parts of the world as well because Holland is the main marketplace. We buy a lot direct from suppliers*

Advice to other
ENTREPRENEURS

Make sure you have a good
network of support.

there and just use the Covent Garden market to top up. We can have a big hotel we have to do flowers for and we don't want to have to run and spend two hours in the market, gathering all the things we want. We order it two days before and it's delivered, so it's fantastic as far as we're concerned.

Jane is still ambitious for the future and has many things she would like to accomplish, including expanding the business into more product lines and having her own vase selection and fragrance range.

These are all things we have tried to do several times along the way but unless you have somebody who can get those products into the stores for you, there's no point in going off and spending money to make a wonderful product if there's no distribution to the people who will buy it.

She admits she doesn't hanker after the old days of traipsing around the flower markets.

You grow and move on, and no one would want to do exactly the same job for 25 years. You need to move on. Sometimes I still do go to the markets and its lovely and I end up buying masses of flowers for myself, so it's reassuring – still having that love for them – and finding the new things that come along are exciting.

Jane Packer Flowers now has two stores in London, including a concession in Harvey Nichols in Knightsbridge, and outlets in New York, Tokyo and Seoul. Jane's dream is to get her stores into Italy and retire there. She admits the buzz for her is not about jumping on a plane and running somewhere new any more but that 'the excitement is seeing the business develop. When I started, floristry wasn't fabulously fashionable at all. It's amazing to be part of that.'

Asked if she could do it all again, Jane is emphatic in her positive response. 'I came from a very small town in Essex, and my life now is very different from what I expected. Subsequently, my children's life will be very different. I've changed the direction of what was expected of me.'

toptable.co.uk

Karen Hanton

'**M**aybe David Beckham has a hotline to the Ivy', says Karen Hanton when pondering the difficulties most mere mortals experience in securing tables at the most sought-after eateries.

The founder of the UK's biggest online restaurant booking service launched her company in February 2000. Operating out of a central London office with a staff of 58, this year toptable.co.uk will seat four million diners and bring over £100m worth of revenue to the restaurant industry. Food for thought indeed.

'I couldn't do anything I didn't believe in and use myself', she says of her passion for her latest venture. 'I see us as the marketing arm of the restaurant industry.'

Karen was brought up on a 35-acre smallholding just outside Aberdeen and came to London in the late 1970s.

'If you'd said to anyone then "oh Karen will have some modest success in business" they'd probably have burst out laughing', she says.

Whilst building her first career in Personnel Management, she worked part-time in bars and as an usherette at the Kensington Odeon cinema. 'I don't think I'd like to go back to that though', she laughs, 'I remember seeing the Odessa File 63 times and that was a bit of a drag.'

Karen says the impetus to get started with toptable was spotting an opportunity where she found herself in need of a way of marketing a restaurant venture she became involved in by accident. She had worked on a number of start-ups and developed companies to various levels; the most recent prior to toptable being a recruitment company Mortimer and Spinks, which she eventually sold to a FTSE 250 company in 1997.

'I was then involved by accident in a restaurant venture and needed a way of promoting it.' Using the internet seemed a logical solution. 'And maybe', she remembers thinking, 'other restaurants could join me and promote their restaurants under one umbrella. Voila 'toptable'. So having sworn I would never do another start up, toptable was unleashed in February 2000. When will I ever learn?' she laughs in mock despair.

'We worked in my house, probably until there were about 10 of us', she says of starting her business, literally, from her kitchen table in London's Victoria. 'The man of my house said to me after a while that whilst he didn't mind living in a commune, it was getting ridiculous! He went to work and by the time he arrived home, they'd still be there. He'd cook dinner for all of us and sometimes even breakfast and lunch too! We had two telephone lines and had to queue up to use them. We had one PC and a dot matrix printer. I'm not sure it's always right to do start-ups quite like that, but it definitely was in our case at that time.'

After that first year in her own home, they had a space problem, which Karen neatly resolved by buying the vacant mews house next door. 'It might sound like I'm well off, but I bought it with a large mortgage. It doesn't mean you actually have the money!'

The team spent three years there before moving into their current offices. Karen, who had also worked in Human Resources for several years, found the experience invaluable when hiring and managing her own team.

'I think management is really applied psychology', she explains. 'Understanding what makes us all tick and how we react towards one another is the basis of most managers. It's a bit like a football team – you have to put

toptable.co.uk can find you the perfect table for two

together a set of complementary skills and understand what buttons to hit in each person to get the best out of them and to help them unlock their own potential. So it has been helpful having my background.'

Since toptable's inception, Karen estimates she has, to date, invested a seven figure sum of her own money ('I kind of got a surprise when I realised it was so much!') together with investment from friends and associates.

I certainly didn't go into it thinking I'd have to put that much in. It crept up on me. I got to a point where I thought that I had put too much into this to lose it and that I had to make it work. I had to find it wherever I could because I'm not an independently wealthy person. We still have a very frugal mentality even though the company has been profitable for a couple of years. I think it's in my genes because I come from a croft in Scotland so my natural approach to things is to do it on a sensible budget.

Most of the money went on website creation, technology and hiring the right staff.

Notable shareholders include Gary Rhodes and Sir Alex Ferguson, who she describes as 'probably the greatest manager of all time.'

It took a 'very scary' five years to turn a profit. Was there ever a time when she felt she'd bitten off more than she could chew?

'I suppose', she reasons, 'toptable.co.uk is a testament to the team who refused to accept that this business would go the same way as most of the others started up at the same time. Let's face it: we started practically on the day of the dot-com bust. Either we are very determined or just plain bloody minded and can't give up!'

Karen did some market research, but 'not a huge amount. To be truthful we talked to a handful of restaurants and said "oh if we posted a few tables on our website would you pay us £1 for everyone we sent" sort of thing', she says. 'They said yes so we knew we had "stock" for sale.'

Whilst she did prepare some financials, she says they undershot the sales targets so dramatically that they were soon abandoned. Instead, they 'concentrated on taking every desperate measure we could think of to survive. But that was in the beginning and for many years we have had quite detailed business plans. We use them religiously as our roadmap; you have to so that everyone can aim at the same goal.'

Getting the first restaurants on board was difficult, 'and I don't blame them either', says Karen, 'because it was a totally new concept in restaurant bookings. Restaurants had never given any of their tables to anyone else to sell, so they were very nervous about it. The only way we could get them to say 'yes' to work with us was to say that we would do it on a results basis.'

Today the business model is still simple: toptable is paid a commission of £2 per 'seat' every time they send someone to a restaurant. It is free to the consumer.

'The whole concept of booking restaurants online works; whether it's to check out a menu, get a free meal for booking half a dozen times, or being a restaurant critic', she

<table><tr><td>Role MODEL

Sir Martin Sorrell at WPP. He went on to build a massive, global business all very quietly without too much in the way of shouting from the rooftops. But then again you could say Branson has done the same but with lots of shouting from the rooftops.</td></tr></table>

says. 'We ask everyone who has made a booking to pretend they're AA Gill and we get over 1,000 reviews every day! I love this but it is a logistical nightmare.'

With toptable sending every single piece of feedback to the restaurants, Karen believes they act as a mini-consultancy; giving restaurants information about their customers they wouldn't normally have – one of the good things about 'having a middle man between restaurants and consumers.'

Karen knew she had developed a 'proper' business when the company started to turn a profit in 2005. She says the reason for toptable's popularity is simple:

> As people have become more accustomed to doing things online, it fits very well with the leisure and lifestyle tools that everyone else is using. Booking travel, hotels, and cars – you can just about live your whole life on the web. Behind the web, hopefully, they realise is a nice fluffy team of people.

Karen admits to finding anything to do with promoting herself personally rather embarrassing:

> I would much rather promote the business. My job is quite a lot about flying the toptable flag more than anything else as well as a bit of strategy and international development. But any good PR will tell you that people like

Advice to other ENTREPRENEURS

Don't underestimate the commitment it needs – it will take longer to get off the ground than you think (normally) and try to make sure you don't make your husband/wife/partner live it day to day, too.

a human story and so this tends to be why quite often an individual is thrust into the limelight. I also think the 'woman succeeds' story is quite a popular one. I am delighted that after seven years, the toptable brand has some standing but you can never afford to sit on your laurels.

Karen doesn't believe in having regrets in business:

Frankly, it is fatal to look back with remorse, as you can't change stuff. But it is vital to learn from your mistakes. And believe me, everyone makes them. I think if anything I would like to have had more belief in myself when I was younger as I have sometimes doubted my judgement on certain things.

She says she doesn't feel challenged by traditional perceptions of what women 'should' be doing. However, she believes women sometimes have to make difficult choices.

It strikes me that more value could be placed on being a full-time parent and for people not to feel under so much pressure to be in business – finances permitting of course. I made a decision that I would dedicate a large part of my life to business and chose not to have children, as I knew I would find it hard to tear myself away from them when working long hours. I do admire women who do it all but I just couldn't. I have met some really impressive women who are single parents and run incredible businesses. How do they manage I wonder?

As for those women who do decide to go for their business dream, she tells them not to underestimate the commitment it needs. 'It will take longer to get off the ground than you think and you must try to make sure you don't make your partner live it day to day, too. Chances are they have their own set of worries in their job, and downloading all of yours 24/7 can put tremendous pressure on a relationship', she advises.

In recognition of her entrepreneurial efforts, Karen was awarded the *Financial Times*/Moet Hennessy Extraordinary Achievers Award in 2000 and named as one of today's top 30 entrepreneurs by a business magazine.

Toptable.co.uk has received a number of awards. It was named one of the top 50 websites for foodies by *The Independent* newspaper, and in both 2006 and 2007 was named in the top 50 fastest growing new media companies in the UK in the prestigious Media Momentum Awards.

In 2006, the company purchased the City-Eating Group, a network of 61 global food websites including the well-known brand www.london-eating.co.uk. Like toptable.co.uk, it receives over one million visitors per month.

Profits are reinvested into the business across technology, marketing and international projects and the company also currently work in Paris, Barcelona, Rome, Berlin and New York. Of the latter, Karen jokes 'I keep saying to people here, "are you sure we don't need an office there? I'll happily go set it up!"'

Toptable isn't a job to Karen. It's more a way of life, although she says she's not a workaholic; 'I love the country, animals and travelling. I set up a charitable trust specifically for animal causes which helps support amazing people doing tremendous work so that animals have a better quality of life.'

Looking ahead, she believes toptable.co.uk could develop even further globally, building on early success in other markets including France, Spain, Germany, Italy and the US.

Of all the businesses that I have worked on, I think this one has the most potential. When I started the business, I definitely did think in terms of an exit plan a few years later. But to tell you the truth, I can't see an end to this one at the moment. One, because I do think it has even greater global possibilities, and two, because I love this business a lot and it would be very difficult to part with it and my wonderful team.

JoJo Maman Bébé

Laura Tenison MBE

'**M**aternity', says Laura Tenison thoughtfully, 'is a terrible market.'

Still, the 40-year old Welsh-born mother of two has made it work for her. Established in 1993, JoJo Maman Bébé is now a multi-channel manufacturer and retailer of maternity and childrenswear, nursery products, gifts and toys.

Laura has an impressive array of awards, including Welsh Entrepreneur of the Year 2003, Laura's 2004 MBE for services to business and the *Harper's and Queen* magazine Entrepreneur of the year 2005.

Operating out of a design studio in London with the head office in Newport, South Wales, JoJo has around 240 staff and 20 stores nationwide, with a further eight opening annually.

Laura went into the business alone and admits she is totally self-taught. Her business beginnings are typical of many women entrepreneurs. Looking for a new challenge, she spotted a gap in the clothing production market.

'I didn't invest any capital initially – I didn't have any. I used the proceeds from the sale of my previous sole-trader business (working as a French Property Agent), which was around £50,000. We took three years to become profitable.'

JoJo has grown from a startup business to one with around £15m turnover without requiring excessive borrowing or outside investors. But when considering how long she spent on her first business plan, Laura chokes on her coffee. 'Only a day.' she admits.

'However', she says, 'considering how tiny the startup company was, I carried out a significant amount of market research – far too much in fact.' She also went to her bank manager for very basic business plan advice. The business plan is now far more complicated; '100 pages with proper budgets, cash flows and profit and loss forecasts.' Laura laughs as she looks at her original one-page cash flow forecasts for 1993.

She admits her biggest challenge was financing the business and learning a new industry from scratch. 'It would', she laughs, 'have been helpful to have had some training!'

Laura did a sewing O level and learned to cut patterns by taking garments to pieces. When she was trying to make clothes commercially, she went to factories and asked people for advice. There were stages when she wishes she had taken a clothing production course before launching into business.

It would have sped things up in the early years since I would have known from the start basic principles like the function of a garment technologist, the detail required on a factory specification sheet or how to produce a proper grading spreadsheet. However I've yet to employ someone who has learnt everything I needed to know on one course. I also think it would have been useful to have more knowledge of financials; I did spend a couple of days with the Prince's Trust learning basic business skills which allowed me to keep the books for the first two years of trading, but it wasn't really enough.

The company only hired a bookkeeper when it was turning over £800,000 and Tenison admits to creating a few confusions along the way:

Each VAT return I seemed to find a new system for my calculations, so when we finally had an inspection after two years of trading, I couldn't remember

Maternitywear by JoJo Maman Bébé

how I'd worked them all out, but I knew the figures were right! The VAT man spent a week with us, painstakingly deciphering my mess. He finally admitted that despite my unorthodox bookkeeping our only error was an overpayment of £56!

Laura also failed to register her company name correctly. Whilst she registered it at Companies House, she neglected to register it as a trademark. Four years on, she was sued by another company for infringement of their trademark. The lesson was an expensive one, costing her £26,000 to defend herself.

'Learning by your mistakes is an expensive way to start a business but you certainly become proficient in every area of your company and you make sure you don't make the same mistake twice', she says.

Laura admits to keen moments of self-doubt in the three years it took to turn a profit, describing those times as a 'complete and utter nightmare'.

For two years the company was struggling. Yes, we had fantastic orders coming in but keeping up with the demand was virtually impossible. When a company grows this quickly you need to relocate to larger premises time and time again, which means unexpectedly adding to your overheads. In addition we realised we needed to sit on large quantities of stock to supply the unpredictable surges in demand.

After two years, the pound devalued and JoJo's cost prices increased dramatically. It was a real crunch point for Tenison, as she had to decide whether to put her house on the line. She had to ask herself whether she really believed in her company or not. She subsequently remortgaged at a time when equity was dire.

At that stage, I had to think very carefully – do I give in or do I invest again in the company and bail it out? It was tough sustaining those levels of energy and enthusiasm after three years of working round the clock on a minimal salary but I believed the company could succeed. Until we turned over £5m, my parents kept asking when I was going to get a proper job – self belief, even if it is just a show, is essential in those startup years. There was definitely an attitude that I was wasting time and I'd given up a perfectly good job to pursue my own business.

As the business started, Laura remembers doing everything herself with the whole company operating out of a room the size of her current office. They even shared with another start-up company.

We listened to Radio 4 to keep us sane whilst inputting customer data. Our customers must have been surprised to hear The Archers theme tune in the background as they placed their orders. I like running a larger company but I do miss not knowing all the employees as well as I used to. I meet them when we set up a new store, but I can't get to know everyone and work alongside them as I did in the past – there just isn't time. I spend a little time at our new stores at the opening and during the visual merchandising – but even with only 30 stores, I am only able to get round each store about once a year. I am already on the road so much, finding new locations and visiting factories and suppliers.

Role MODEL

My role model has to be Bob Geldof. I love the fact that he gets things done without fuss and prevarication. He is talented, intelligent, funny, hardworking, business-minded and a good parent – what more could one want?

Laura initially wanted to launch a childrenswear company but in order to follow her market research, results had to begin with maternity. From her experiences abroad in Brittany, she knew she wanted to do something based on the Breton t-shirt style. 'I love the French nautical look', she explains. 'Without being too obvious, our stores are light and airy and should give a healthy but pure feel. We have a handmade wooden shop fit which works really well with our predominantly nautical baby and children's collection. We appeal to active families who love the idea of putting their baby in a carrier and going for walks on the beach.'

Laura turns to a filing cabinet and brings out a fluffy rabbit. 'This is JoJo,' she says smiling.

JoJo is a brand name that I thought would work for mothers and babies. But JoJo is also this little rabbit whose mother unfortunately is a businesswoman who never has enough time for him and multi-tasks too much. I created JoJo (and wrote a children's book about him) 10 years ago, partly tongue in cheek to pacify my baby son and partly to satisfy the queries of 'who is JoJo?' Also we needed a new logo design and I thought it would be quite fun to develop our own mascot.

Laura is nothing if not practical and is preparing a disaster recovery plan in the event of her death. It may be slightly morbid, but Laura believes that you have to think that far ahead. 'I say it's the housekeeper in me, the organised woman in me trying to multi-task, and you have to foresee every eventuality.'

She's also passionate about respecting her suppliers. The company spends time and energy building up good relationships, partly because she believes in courteous business practice, but also as a reminder to herself of the problems she had finding good factories in the early years.

One of our first supply sources was Columbia in South America. For my first collection I had a portfolio of designs, which I was taking around factories trying to find a manufacturer. I wanted to make 50 pieces in a style and I couldn't get anyone to make that sort of quantity for the price points I needed. At a trade fair in Paris, I happened to see, tucked away in a dusty corner, this row of Columbian manufacturers who were being funded by the EEC to promote non-drugs trade. They were stuck in a hopeless position at the back of the hall and were getting little passing trade.

Laura showed them her designs, told them her pricing criteria and was on a plane to Columbia the following week. Her husband, a criminal-defence barrister, was horrified by the implications of importing from Columbia, but the relationship worked very well. 'However', says Laura, 'it was only by my going to the factories, telling them my vision, sitting next to the machinists and showing them how to make the clothes to the right standard that I got the production line off the ground.'

JoJo now buys from 200 different companies, and their target is to visit 90% of their suppliers during the year.

A consultant looking at our business model might tell us to dump three quarters of our suppliers. However, I feel the extra time and expense is well worth it. We offer hand-knitted ponchos made in Peru by cottage industry. Not many retailers can sustain trading with a supplier on this level but we persevere. Of course a large number of small suppliers eats into our overheads, reducing our profit margins, but this level of diversity is our USP and is appreciated by our customers.

Laura is proud that 14 years on, they are still working with the same factories she started trading with. She does her best to stay loyal, believing they rely on JoJo as much as JoJo relies on them.

Whilst we are not a big company, our orders can still make a real difference to a small factory. Regular and guaranteed production will sustain a factory and its workforce. Some of our production bases are very small and if we took our business away, then they would struggle and maybe have to close. It is tragic to watch the fickle way that the clothing industry is moving from country to country as new, cheaper markets open up. Too many retailers shift production from season to season, putting their work out to tender regardless of the devastation it can cause. We try to get across to our customers that we put ethical business practices above profit. Our retail prices may be slightly more than the supermarkets, but we aim for a lower profit margin; so the customers and the company are sharing the costs of producing in an environmental and ethical manner.

Laura makes a point of keeping her eyes open for new design ideas, rushing home to sketch them up as soon as inspiration hits. She readily admits that she can occasionally irritate the designers by 'putting my oar in' with her insistence that they do, for example, a cashmere hat with flaps when the team are equally adamant they don't need one. 'Sometimes I get some resistance to my ideas, but generally I can get a design pushed through – an advantage of being the MD!' she says.

When it comes to the mail-order side of the business, Laura stresses the huge importance of analysing the database, which she describes as the most valuable part of any mail-order company. She estimates that JoJo has 1.5 million names, which are carefully segmented into around 30 groups.

Advice to other
ENTREPRENEURS

Only launch a business if you have the stamina to work 20 hours a day, for no money, for three years.

'We look at customer buying patterns; those who are multiple buyers, sale buyers only, those who are offer buyers only and will buy once and never again. Caution is essential', she warns. 'A catalogue costs around 80p to print and mail. If you're mailing out hundreds of thousands a year and they're not well targeted, you're going to go out of business quite quickly.'

The company codes every piece of advertising so they can track back and work on converting advertising spend into orders.

Laura is passionate about encouraging the regeneration of local high streets and would prefer to keep the retail stores out of shopping centres.

We don't want people to think of us as a predatory chain that is chasing the independent shopkeeper off the high street like some of the supermarkets. We obviously are a small chain now, but we are still an independent retailer and train our store managers to run the stores as if they were owner managers. Naturally they are targeted so it is in their interests to sell, but they have leeway to run their own stores in their own way as long as their methods involve exceptional customer service. Our customers should feel comfortable to come into the store for advice and a chat whenever they are passing.

Financially, the split between purchases online, in store and via catalogue is roughly equal. 'More or less, 33% each', says Laura. 'This current year, our turnover is £5m mail order; £5m web mail order and £5m stores. We aim for a 5% profit margin, whilst your average retailer will aim for a 10–15% profit margin. That's the way we want to work; I'm more interested in brand building and customer satisfaction than profit.'

Indeed, Laura admits to paying herself 'a tenth' of what she probably could for running a £15m turnover company, because she wants to invest in the long-term future of the business.

Undeniably a hugely successful career woman, Laura is very much aware of the downside of being a woman in business and warns those toying with the idea of setting up on their own that it is far from easy and involves extremely long hours. 'If you want an easy life, then work for someone else', she advises.

She says her biggest sacrifice was taking no maternity leave after the birth of her two children, Ben (11) and Toby (7). 'I went back to work straight after each birth – although the babies did come with me from time to time and were both conveniently born on Fridays, giving me the weekend to recover.'

She's also expected to be the house-maker and it's her responsibility to take on the majority of the childcare as her husband's job takes him all over the country.

I have to make sure that business and family life work in tandem without one of them damaging the other. Had I not had a family, life would have been much easier. Had I been a man with a supportive stay-at-home wife, life would have been great. But I chose to have a family, a business and a husband and now I have to make sure they all get enough attention. Sometimes it feels like you have to be superwoman without ever mentioning any problems to anyone. If you want to 'have it all', you need more energy than most to make sure nothing gives. Very few people understand how difficult it is. You have to accept that you're not going to get any sleep because the only time left to get those targets written up for the 9am meeting is when everyone else has gone to bed. I refuse to miss out on anything but being a mother, wife and MD is hard, very hard. Despite this I wouldn't have it any other way.

————— *JW* —————

Leila Wilcox

Leila Wilcox believes that determination and a will to succeed are the keys to success. The founder of award-winning children's toiletries range, Halos n Horns, began trading in August 2005 and broke even in her first month. Originally based in Oxford and Soho, the company started with a devoted staff of five.

Leila is one of a fast-growing band of women entrepreneurs who have based their business idea around a personal need. Appalled by the chemical concoctions in her son's shampoos and bath washes, she issued a challenge to the major players in the industry by removing all the harmful chemicals linked to eczema, asthma and contact dermatitis from her own range.

Both concerned mother and savvy entrepreneur, Leila believes her dual roles are interlinked. 'All products in the Halos n Horns range carry a message from me to other mothers as I created the brand to satisfy my own requirements as a young mum; those of finding safe, fun and affordable toiletries for my son Troy.'

By all accounts, the message has been well received, by mothers and retailers alike. The range of shampoos and body washes, with kid-friendly names like Zingy Orange, Halo Baby and Melon Mango Mayhem, is stocked in Waitrose, Tesco, Morrisons, Ocado, Superdrug and Asda. 'We cover almost every retailer now', she says.

The Baby Bath is her favourite product, purely for sentimental reasons: Troy was just a baby himself when she first started the business. 'I still use it as bubble bath and shower gel', she says.

The original idea for the range of children's shampoos came from a hairdressing friend, Joe Mills, owner of The Lounge Soho hair boutiques. Leila further developed the concept with Ivan Massow, her mentor from the Channel 4 programme, *Make Me a Million*, which she won in November 2005 ('my proudest moment to date.')

The whole set-up process was continually beset with challenges; getting onto the show, raising the funding, finding a manufacturer, persuading retailers to stock us. But little by little these challenges became hurdles rather than obstacles. Also believing in myself – that I could achieve something as enormous as Halos n Horns.

Indeed, she admits that self-belief and believing in the potential of her product have been her biggest personal challenges in building up the business. So much so that when she first started, she was startled by the fact that strangers were buying her products. Not her friends or family, but actual paying customers who were writing to her and telling her they loved the product. This is where she credits Ivan for his encouragement. He could see the potential and told Leila she could take Halos n Horns worldwide and become an international brand rather than her thinking she could just sell it online.

Leila is contemptuous of how she believes the big industry players use clever marketing to suggest their products are 'kind, gentle and mild' and thinks they use chemicals purely to reduce their production costs. However, she feels validated by the response she has received from parents since launching the range. 'We've received hundreds of emails and letters from worried parents whose children's eczema or dry skin conditions have

Halos n Horns hair and bath products

cleared up since they stopped using major brands and started using ours.'

Leila invested 'every last penny' of her own money in the fledgling business. The rest of the funding came from her family, especially her 'nan' who contributed her life savings.

She spent a large period of time – many months – doing her homework and still does now:

> *One aspect was researching the chemicals contained in other products on the market; the other was interviewing mums and parents in order to determine buying patterns, preferences and opinions. This is how I came up with our USPs; from doing the leg-work and interviewing parents I discovered that they wanted products that are safe, kiddie, fun and yet still affordable. It seemed a tall order at the time, but we achieved it! We also spoke to specialist doctors, paediatricians, dermatologists, midwives and other health professionals.*

Leila has always felt a need to run her own business. 'My father and grandfather have their own businesses, so it's something I've wanted to do', she reveals. 'However, as a young mother it was impossible to imagine I could achieve something as amazing as this.'

She has made a point of drawing inspiration from like-minded women; 'Lynne Franks provided me with great business advice when I started, and Gita Patel, founder of Trapezia – the UK's first investment product to concentrate on women-focused businesses – is part of my team.'

Overall, Leila believes that being a woman in business has been an advantage:

> *We have used the 'one mum to another' message to communicate our brand and if I had been a man this would not have been possible. However, at first I felt disadvantaged. This, I later discovered, was because I was adopting a 'victim mentality' caused by my own insecurities. Once I stopped that mindset, I saw my gender as an advantage and played it to the full.*

Leila believes that women can bring a sense of balance and of business ethics, which men are more resistant to due to macho stereotypes and ego constraints. Women, she feels, are much more willing to listen and compromise.

Leila says she has found all of the big supermarket chains 'absolutely fantastic' to deal with.

> *They were not at all like you read in the press, which surprised me. The key to our success was showing how our product could benefit them. We could prove that we'd done our market research; we could prove that parents did want this and we could show how it could benefit them by bringing quality onto the supermarket shelf.*

She is always interested in new developments, from fizz balls to colours, and ways of making the products more and more fun. 'Our main aim is to keep this product very safe and free of the chemicals, so it does restrict us; that's why we make it as fun as possible with the safest ingredients we can.'

Leila's day average day is hectic. The morning of our interview she was woken at 5 am by her son Troy clambering into bed. 'I know I shouldn't have let him, but it was 5 am and I'm not that strong willed I'm afraid!'

She is up again at 7 am, making Troy's packed lunch and dropping him off at nursery before going to the gym for an hour. She's at work for 9 o'clock, working straight through till 5.30 pm when she's back at nursery to collect Troy. She then takes him to the park, nips to Tesco, ('as I seem to do the supermarket run about five times a week!'), makes some dinner, gets him to bed and then finally collapses on the sofa at around 9 pm.

Thanks to a partnership with distribution specialists Ceuta Healthcare, who have handled the everyday running of the business since May 2006, Halos n Horns is currently expanding abroad in Ireland, Malta, New Zealand and Australia.

'We were just constantly getting requests from retailers, the distribution managers and mums for the product to go abroad', says Leila, 'so we thought, we've got to do this. I couldn't continue to develop *and* export *and* get all the products to mums, and the mums were getting frustrated. I was just so bogged down with the day-to-day running of the company that I couldn't do anything to do with brand development, PR or marketing, so now I'm really focusing on where the brand's going and international export.'

Two months after exchanging with Ceuta and just as she was in the process of handing over, Leila broke her back in a serious car accident.

'Actually it meant Ceuta had to take over', she recalls.

I would have probably carried on doing a lot more than I did but because of the crash, they had to. I was lucky, because if it had been a month or two months later, then I don't know what would have happened to the business. I hate to say it, but it probably would have gone bust because I was the only one at that time, before the exchange, who knew who everyone was. I did everything – the whole day-to-day running of the business.

After her accident, she went through a period of around three weeks when she didn't look at her computer or her emails. 'I couldn't work, I lost

Role MODEL

Ivan Massow is my business mentor. I also draw inspiration from like-minded women including Lynne Franks who provided me with great business advice when I started, and Gita Patel, founder of Trapezia – the UK's first investment product to concentrate on women-focused businesses – who is part of my team.

every motivation, I just couldn't get back into it. Luckily Ceuta took over and they didn't need me to have any staff; they took over all the logistics, accountancy and distribution side. Now I just work much more on the top line.'

With physiotherapy and hydrotherapy twice a week for her back and legs, the accident brought everything into sharp focus for Leila, who admits that the business now has a disaster-recovery plan in place:

> *I used to do a lot of motivational speaking but since the car accident I've realised that my favourite place is with my son. As much as I'm running the business, I'm not putting in the same amount of hours and I'm not travelling all over the country. I was flying up to Newcastle to do motivational talks – but I don't want to do that, I want to be at home with my son. I've stepped away to focus on running the business and being at home.*

With Ceuta running the day-to-day end of the business, Leila admits to missing the daily phone calls from the mums but says she still loves to read the daily emails (as many as 80 each day) and hear directly from them that they had bought the product or liked it.

Leila says convincing the 'mums' market to believe in the products has never been an issue.

> *I was just a mum who wanted honest good products for my son and I didn't come at this from a manufacturing point of view. I wasn't a multi-billion pound international company trying to get these mums, I just wanted a product available for my son and other kids like him. We've always operated as a very open, honest company and I think people can see that.*

Advice to other ENTREPRENEURS

Don't try and do everything on your own – create a team, then learn how to set goals and achieve them.

Leila Wilcox still loves her job and what she does; 'I love my life, it's fantastic. I'm so happy. I'm proud and pleased with everything that's happened.'

Her plans include creating a full kid's range, from nit shampoo to spikey hair gel ('all nasty-chemical-free of course!') then producing an adult's range. A suncream range is set to launch in retailers in the spring of 2008. 'Eventually I'd like to set up a charity or supportive network for women trying to set up businesses.'

When asked what one piece of advice she would give to other would-be entrepreneurs, Leila Wilcox is clear: 'never give up, and give it your very best. That way you will never have regrets, and with luck, you'll succeed.'

———— *LW* ————

Liz Jackson MBE

If you can't find a company that you want to work for, why not set up your own? It has certainly worked for Liz Jackson, founder and managing director of multi-million-pound telemarketing firm Great Guns Marketing.

Starting as an office junior at local mergers and acquisitions firm BCMS, she had worked her way up, finding her niche in training and developing telemarketers. However, after eight years, Liz was ready for a change. The companies she went to for interview left her feeling uninspired, so deciding she preferred the buzz of a small, entrepreneurial office to a corporate environment, she made a decision. In 1998, aged just 25 and encouraged by her former boss that she could do better, she set up on her own, taking her old company with her as her first client.

Finding the bank's business plan difficult to follow, ('you would have to have got an MA in business to understand it'), she successfully secured a

£1,000 grant and £4,000 loan from the Prince's Trust. Setting up from the living room in her rented flat in Basingstoke, she spent the money wisely, buying a second-hand computer, fax machine, phones and a desk.

'I knew I'd want someone to come and work with me quite quickly', continues Liz, 'so I recruited a second person after about a month and got somebody in working alongside me part time, building it from there.' The first employee was a friend; the second was her mother, whom Liz describes as 'a brilliant telemarketer.'

But Liz soon faced a more serious challenge. Born with a degenerate eyesight condition called retinitis pigmentosa, she had until then been able to lead a relatively normal life. However, the disease became more aggressive and within three months of starting Great Guns Marketing, it left her totally blind.

Whilst she subsequently had to employ someone to read her computer for her and take her out to meetings, Liz is adamant that her condition didn't hamper the running of the business:

Sales are really dependent on personality so it didn't affect me at all. Something like 86% of blind people don't work – there are very few blind people in employment. It is really quite difficult for blind people to get jobs, and employers to have the grace and understanding. Having said that, I don't think many of them apply for jobs either – people's confidence gets knocked. I'm really pleased I set up the business at the time I did, and I think if I'd gone blind, I probably would have been more likely to set up my own company, as opposed to having the courage to work for someone else.

Liz admits she didn't spend too long on deciding on the name of the business. 'I went out to dinner with a friend and when we got back to my flat, we drank a bottle of red wine. I was throwing names around and said "what happens when people say you're doing really well? They say you're going great guns – let's call it Great Guns Marketing." That was after "Birds Do Business" and all sorts of ridiculous ones. That was the most sensible one to come out!'

Liz developed Great Guns Marketing as a niche telemarketing company, specifically focusing on making b2b (business-to-business) appointments.

'We do have some really good competitors, and I actually really appreciate them, which is a funny thing to say', says Liz. 'But we drum up business for each other quite often – because we're cold-calling businesses all the time

Talking the talk: Great Guns telemarketers

to introduce Great Guns, and if someone's serious about telemarketing, they'll often ring one of our other competitors as well, to compare us. I'd much rather have good competitors than bad ones. You always have to be better than them; you are constantly looking at the way you service your clients, training your people, processes and procedures. All of those things are on a constant improvement curve. If we were the only company doing it, it probably wouldn't have grown or developed as much.'

With customer service key, hiring the right staff is crucial for Liz. Any potential Great Guns employee needs to display a real passion for the business and an understanding of its vision and expectations:

What I've found is the best way to get loyalty is to get people to really buy into what we are trying to achieve, and to make them feel that they're really important, and that what they do really contributes to what we do as a company. If they are low skilled, you can train that, but attitude you can't really – attitude is really, really important. I think from a quality point of view that's what I'm really looking for: people with a great work ethic and attitude.

Whilst clearly committed to her staff and to growing the company, Liz admits that business has never been her whole life. Family comes first and it has been important to her to encourage a supportive and warm working environment at the office.

When you run a family business, everyone who works for you does become part of the clan really. Being at work doesn't feel like perhaps some offices can feel. I've always had four holidays a year, worked a nine-to-five day and never worked weekends since I started it ten years ago – even in the early stages.

In 2002 and keen to move the business on, Liz sought advice from her client The Franchise Company. She set about franchising her own business, viewing it as the best way of branching out regionally and building a national brand.

'For a start', says Liz, 'it made it a lot more cost effective for me than literally opening/renting premises, employing people and all the rest of it. And you got a better quality of person, someone who was entrepreneurial, but wanted the ability to set up and run a business without having to go through all the learning curves themselves. So it worked out really well.'

The development was not, however, without its problems.

It's quite difficult finding the right people to run franchises. When you think that 80% of businesses fail in year one, although franchising completely betters your odds, you still have to get people who have that determination. A lot of people we have interviewed for franchises seem to have a 'get rich quick' mentality. Do you remember pyramid selling? I get the impression that people set up businesses with this idea of the promise of pyramid selling – 'this time next year, you'll be a millionaire'. It just doesn't happen like that! It's really hard work. Running a business, you've got to have pretty thick skin and you have got to keep trying and going. There are a lot of people who just give in at the first hurdle.

Although they currently have seven regional offices, including Glasgow, Waterford and Birmingham, Liz admits Great Guns has had franchises that just haven't worked out, mainly because they appointed the wrong person.

Liz relies on a trusted circle of company directors for advice and support, including both her parents: her father as commercial director and her mother heading up Human Resources.

Instead of making decisions on my own, very much based on intuition, I tend to consider things and bounce ideas off those guys now a bit more. We also measure and monitor everything a lot more than we used to – just because the figures are so much bigger. By splitting up the job, and being able to delegate areas of the business to those people, I have been able to spend more time working on the business, instead of being in it.

Liz says that telemarketing is a feminine business and those clichéd perceptions of a woman on the telephone with a great big smile actually work in her favour.

'When I sit down in front of someone round a boardroom table and start talking about telemarketing, I think I come across as someone with a lot of credibility as straight away they're thinking "yes, she does sound like a telemarketer!"'

Great Guns has opened up many doors for Liz; she is frequently in demand for her brand of inspirational conference and dinner-speaking, and met Jacqueline Gold at the International Entrepreneurs Conference in Dubai.

In 2003, Liz won the Women Mean Business Award and in 2004, Great Guns Marketing won the South East Regional Customer Focus Award. Most recently, Liz received an MBE for services to business.

'Obviously it's built the brand', says Liz. 'A lot of companies that hear me speak call us up and say "can you help us with telemarketing?" It's been brilliant to be honest.'

Frank and forthright, she's thoughtful when considering the 'secrets' of her success and honest in assessing why she personally appeals across such a broad audience:

Role MODEL

I aspire to all sorts of different people, especially anyone who has overcome a barrier to hit a goal.

I suppose in a way people probably look at me, and think 'she's 33, blind, academically rubbish, and just a telemarketer, and yet she's been able to do that.' It probably gives people hope that they could do it. Because I'm not an intellect, I don't come from an academic background and I don't have an MA in business or any of those things, I think I probably talk very simply and just about anyone can understand. The really clever people find me slightly amusing, and the people that are a bit more like me find me inspirational. People just think 'if she can do it, I'll have a go.'

A committed Christian, Liz believes her beliefs have made running a business much easier. She says she has never lost any sleep over running her company and finds prayer comforting.

It relinquishes responsibility a bit because you think it's kind of God's responsibility in some respects. If he wants me to keep doing what I'm doing, then he'll look after me. You tend to feel like you've got somebody on your side, fighting your corner for you. It makes it easy to make decisions as well – it is either right or wrong. If you are making decisions on how you run your business and you have to make ethical decisions, it's quite black and white really. It's either honest or it's not; it's either the right thing or it's not. You probably take more risks, because you think 'the big guy's on my side, I can't go wrong.'

Great Guns Marketing currently has around 700 clients across the UK and a turnover in excess of £2.5m. Employing about 100 staff, they recently opened another franchise in Cambridge. 'A woman franchisee, which is fabulous!' says Liz delightedly.

Advice to other
ENTREPRENEURS

Get the right staff!

The plan is to have up to 16 franchises across the UK and then turn the company's attention overseas.

She has just become a mother for the first time and wasn't able to take maternity leave. Instead, she plans to work two to three days a week until her daughter is three years old.

I've given 10 years to my business, and have built it to the level that it's at now. She is going to be my priority until she goes to school, then I will do nine to three. I really want to be a mum. I won't get this chance again; she's only going to be a baby once. She will come with me, whilst she can, and when she can't, I won't do it. The business runs really, really well but you don't have to be there nine to five every day. I've worked really hard to get to where it is; I'm going to spend the time with her now.

———————— *IW* ————————

Perween Warsi MBE

A **bad experience** with a samosa is never pleasant. However, for 51-year old Perween Warsi, the outcome was more positive: it inspired her to launch one of the UK's most successful, independent food retailing companies.

'S&A Foods started out from my home kitchen, and has grown into what it is today through hard work, determination and high-quality products', she says.

S&A Foods supplies major retailers including Asda and clients in the foodservice sector, with international ready meals. Based in Derby, the company has 750 staff and a turnover of £65m.

Born in India, the mother of two sons, Sadiq and Abid (hence S&A) set up her business in 1986:

I was expecting to be able to recreate my own Indian dishes with the ingredients I could buy in the UK, but when I realised that it was very difficult to buy good-quality Indian food it triggered a thought in my mind that maybe I could make a difference. Until that time, I hadn't thought that I would run my own business. I always enjoyed cooking, but just for my family and friends.

Appalled by the quality of Indian food she sampled, she realised this could be her chance. 'After tasting what the supermarkets and local takeaways had to offer I thought that there was an opportunity for high quality, authentic Indian foods in the British marketplace', she recalls. 'I could see where I had the opportunity, and where I eventually wanted to see my products, on the shelves of the British supermarkets.'

From that moment, it became Perween's mission to provide genuine, delicious Indian food to the British public.

Deciding her best course of action was the direct route, she prepared some of her own samosas and convinced a local Indian takeaway to try them. They sold well and Perween began supplying the outlet on a regular basis; six samosas for just £2.50.

Encouraged by this first small success, she approached other takeaways and local delicatessens whilst expanding her range to include finger foods such as chapattis and pakora.

With Perween working 16–18 hour days, S&A Foods grew, and she took on a team of five women to help her in the kitchen. However, supplying to the local trade was never going to be enough for Perween. Her eye was always on the bigger prize: supplying the big retailers.

She began calling supermarkets, persisting until S&A was asked to take part in blind tasting sessions at Asda and Safeway. Her food triumphed over other more established food manufacturers, and the supermarkets called to place an order for Perween's chilled and frozen dishes. There was, however, one small fly in the ointment.

'When Asda offered me the contract', recalls Perween, 'they assumed that S&A Foods was a fully fledged food, manufacturing business. Actually at that time I was still making the dishes in my kitchen, so we had to build up the business, and quickly!'

Perween was determined to create authentic Indian dishes

She admits she had no clue how to move forward:

I had absolutely no plan, no idea whatsoever. I was totally naïve. But one thing I always believe in is learning – you are never too old to learn, it is never too late to learn and you must be open-minded to learning. I learnt my way with my customers, my suppliers and my people and brought in the expertise that I didn't have in the business.

Perween says financial constraints were the biggest challenge to growth:

Getting a loan in the early days was almost as challenging as starting your own business. The business was growing at such a rapid rate that it was initially hard to find any secure investment, especially with my limited experience. While chasing investment, it was vital that I continued to manage the day-to-day running of the business in order for it to grow.

Unwilling to lose her lucky break, Perween took a gamble. In 1987, S&A Foods joined the Hughes Food Group with the resulting investment injection allowing them to open their first factory in Derby – a former car valet depot on an industrial estate.

However, in 1990 the Hughes Food Group went into receivership. With the support of venture capitalists 3i, Perween and husband Talib fought to win back their company in a management buyout in November 1991.

Whilst she does not regret any of the decisions she has taken with her company, she found the loss of control following the Hughes Food Group partnership a bitter pill to swallow:

It meant that I lost control of my vision. Although at the time it was good for the business to join with Hughes as it meant we could afford to build a new factory and create 100 extra jobs, I wasn't in control of the direction the business was going. Looking back, I would have preferred to go into partnership with a company who shared the same beliefs and values as I did for S&A. However, in 1991, we regained full control of the business, and its direction.

In her dealings with the supermarket chains, Perween advocates perseverance and a positive attitude:

You need to have something different, unique and better that they currently do not have to add value to their shelves. Obviously, the whole of the supply chain is geared up to manage our customers' needs and requirements. My belief is my business should be tailored to meet my customers and my consumers, not the food production. At the end of the day, you're trying to fulfil the needs of consumers; when they want it, how they want it. That's how you should gear up your business; to deliver those needs.

In 1996, S&A invested £8m in a new, state-of-the-art factory based on the site of the original plant. The increased capacities enabled them to expand; producing meals and accompaniments from China, India, Thailand and Malaysia as well as launch a range of dishes in conjunction with renowned chef Ken Hom.

Perween admits it was tough starting a business as a mother of two children:

I had to juggle my responsibilities as a wife and mother, as well as starting up S&A Foods. As I am a sociable person, many of my friends thought I had gone back to India when I first started, as I spent many hours devoted to the business! Is there ever a perfect balance between work and home life?

The answer is no. I work the hours the business needs to remain successful, but I always make quality time for my family. Now of course my sons are older and don't live at home, but I do have an adorable granddaughter who I like to spend as much time with as I can.

Having managed to juggle work and family, Perween is still adamant that a choice to be a housewife doesn't mean making any less of a contribution to society than a woman in a career.

'In fact', she says, 'the biggest contribution that anyone can make is to bring up a good, decent human being. It is, therefore, unfair to see a housewife as less worthy than a career woman. I think it is important for successful women to be acknowledged and to provide a supportive and mentoring function for other women who are starting out on the long journey to setting up and running their own business, often with a young family or family commitments.'

As the business developed, she realised that finding and surrounding herself with talented people who are experts in their fields was key to its success.

Role MODEL

Anita Roddick. She had a passion for the products she developed and sold, and she believed very much in what she did. She achieved so much with her business, as well as bringing up a family and looking at environmental issues on a large scale. I admire people who help others; her work trying to empower communities in the Third World, as well as her dedication to helping and supporting women in business was inspirational. Most people live for themselves, and the ability to do both is quite rare.

I would also have to say Allan Leighton. He was involved with Asda during the first few years of S&A working with them. He has been very influential in large British businesses, after moving from Asda to the Royal Mail and to Lastminute.com. Alongside Archie Norman, Allan turned Asda around from a business on the verge of failure to a storming success with US giants Wal-Mart.

'Only by making judgements on ability and not by gender', she says, 'have I been able to run the business successfully.'

Whilst S&A Foods now has a European business, supplying to several food service centres in France and Germany, Perween says there's still plenty to achieve.

'We've just started', she says. 'The European market is very big and has massive opportunities. There is plenty to do still in this country – bringing something new and different to what is not available in terms of concept as well as product ideas. The whole wide world is out there for us to grab it if we want to and we'd love to grab it!'

Her advice to other entrepreneurs is to have confidence in yourself and the product or service you are providing;

> *Make sure you've done your homework, be determined and don't give up. The journey of success could be bumpy so make sure you're prepared for that and have the right people around you. Make sure you always remain focused and determined to succeed. There are some excellent support networks out there, such as Women in Business and the Institute of Directors, which can offer support and advice along the way.*

Her success has made Perween the recipient of many prestigious honours, including the Woman Entrepreneur of the World Award in 1996. The company has been listed for five consecutive years as the UK's fastest-growing independent food manufacturer while other accolades include being the 1997 Finalist in the *Sunday Times* Business Awards and having their Chicken Korma voted best-quality Chicken Korma by *BBC Good Food* magazine in 1998. Most recently, S&A Foods, in conjunction with Asda, won the best supermarket spice dish at the British Curry Awards for its Chicken Tikka Masala.

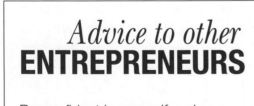

Advice to other
ENTREPRENEURS

Be confident in yourself and your business offering.

Perween is devoted to maintaining the diverse culture at S&A. 'We have 23 languages spoken on the factory floor, and communicate to our staff in many of these', she says, 'We also have a learning centre onsite, which allows employees to learn languages and gain work-related qualifications. It inspires them to reach their potential, both in and out of the workplace.'

When she started the business, Perween spent most of her time either in the factory or seeing customers. Her role today is more focused.

'My job is to work for the strategies of the business – where are we going and how are we going to get there? I have to think if we have the right resources in place and, of course, spend my time with customers. I also spend a lot of my time on product development.'

When Perween started S&A Foods back in 1986, her long-term vision was getting British people to eat authentic Indian cuisines:

It was my crusade, my mission, to make sure that I achieved that – and I feel that by trading through national supermarket chains, we have. Of course, there is a long way to go and more supermarket chains to supply. S&A Foods continues to grow; we are doing more and more business in the UK and across Europe, as well as expanding our food offerings. I am still very much involved on a day-to day basis with S&A Foods. However, I do have a very capable management team surrounding me who I rely on. I still spend time in India, finding out about new flavours and tastes across the country. I think it's important for developing new dishes to actually speak to people, see what they are eating, and what new dishes are coming through.

In 1997, Perween Warsi was awarded an MBE, followed by a CBE in 2002 and a seat on the CBI National Committee. Critically, in 2004, she finally regained 100% control of the business, and in 2005, received the ultimate accolade, the first Women Lifetime Achievement Award.

'All these', she says, 'were amazing experiences, and I would say my proudest achievements for both myself and my family. I have always been known to challenge 'the norm'. When I was a little girl I begged my parents to send me to boarding school – something unusual then for a girl growing up in India. My determination to set up and grow S&A Foods was, for me, pursuing a dream, and I wasn't prepared to let anything stop me from turning that dream into a reality. Of course, I needed to make sure that my family always came first, but they have always been very supportive of my business, which has given me the strength and determination to continue.'

COFFEE REPUBLIC

Sahar Hashemi

A couple of granules of information for you to percolate before we steam ahead:

- Being an entrepreneur was the furthest thing from Sahar Hashemi's mind.
- The chain of coffee bars she co-founded with brother Bobby in 1995 was very nearly called Java Express.
- Her favourite caffeine fix? 'A skinny latte, always', she says firmly.

Sahar and Bobby were behind the original trend for the UK high street coffee chain. A former lawyer, Sahar had become dissatisfied with her career, whilst Bobby, a successful investment banker in New York, was treading water whilst searching for his own big business idea.

The defining moment was the death of their beloved father in 1993, which led them to question where they were going with their own lives. But it was a chance comment at a restaurant in November 1994 which proved the catalyst; Sahar had recently returned from New York and was lamenting London's lack of espresso bars providing proper cappuccinos and muffins. Bobby suddenly remembered that a prospectus of a US chain of coffee bars had recently crossed his desk so he knew that a market existed for them and, in a Eureka moment, he literally woke up and smelt the coffee.

Initially, Sahar was reticent. Just because she loved her coffee didn't mean she had to go and set up her own business selling it. Bobby suggested that she work for him for a week, researching the idea. Having nothing to lose, she agreed.

'Women are the ultimate consumers', she says. 'As shoppers we see what's out there in the market and what's missing – we're in touch. It's an advantage, as a gap in our own lives is often a gap in the market.'

She spent a day on the Circle Line, getting off at each of the 27 stops to investigate what was on offer. She soon realised there was a huge demand for proper coffee. Whilst it was being sold in large quantities everywhere she looked, the quality was poor, presentation was horrendous and the coffee itself seemed to be an afterthought in comparison to the other food and beverages on offer. From that moment, she was utterly dedicated to creating a true, authentic coffee drinking experience, complete with baristas, delicious snacks and warm, welcoming ambience.

They did their research meticulously, speaking to suppliers, coffee machine manufacturers, looking up shop fitters in the *Yellow Pages*, sourcing potential sites and even embarking on a free coffee-making course.

'When we started, I was naïve. It all had a certain mystery to it and my attitude was "life is an adventure"', Sahar recalls. 'It is much easier and nicer being two people. You have to be very lucky to have a good partner. I was lucky with Bobby.'

Her biggest challenge was changing the habits and mindsets of a nation of tea-drinkers; 'not just *selling* a new idea in a market that didn't know what a skinny latte was, but persuading everyone that it was going to work and there would be a market for it', she says.

Bobby and Sahar were rebutted by 22 high street banks. But they kept on going until they secured a £100,000 loan that was backed by the DTI Small Firms Loan Guarantee Scheme.

Sahar is focusing her energies on her new business, Skinny Candy, a range of sugar-free confectionery

'That's my motto', says Sahar, 'you have to keep notching up on those "no's" until you get there.'

'When I started', she continues, 'the word "entrepreneur" didn't exist. Back then, there was just Sir Richard Branson and Anita Roddick. Now there's a lot of support for entrepreneurs. A lot has changed. We live in a world where technology has enabled us to break barriers between work and home. You can work from home and that makes a lot of difference to women entrepreneurs. The whole idea that you can be connected wherever you are gives you flexibility to be a mum and have a family.'

Sahar soon concluded that business was not about finance. 'Women get scared by that', she says. 'Starting a business means using the tools you have in everyday life. With Coffee Republic, what I was surprised about was that buying a shop was like buying a flat: check it, what's the price, get a budget, how much can you afford and what kind of furniture are you going to get?'

The huge, established competitors in the coffee industry never intimidated her. 'Maybe it's just an attitude of mind', she says. 'I just got on with my own idea and my own vision. I think it would be very daunting if one did say, "oh, I'm up against the big boys" because you would never do anything. So I just focus on what I can focus on. Starbucks were strong competitors with more might than us – so what happened was what would in any market environment.'

Sahar adored the time spent starting the business with Bobby; 'you work very hard but you're never counting the hours you work. I always choose careers that I find very fun and where I can be myself, so I'm never really sure when I'm working and when I'm not working!'

They knew they wanted the company name to encapsulate the entire coffee drinking experience; after several false starts, they settled on 'Coffee Republic'. However, their first attempt at having the logo professionally designed was a disaster and cost them their full-allotted budget of £400. Although the problem was rectified, it meant they then couldn't afford Coffee Republic branded cups. They ended up roping in friends to stick branded stickers on them instead.

When it came to product, Sahar viewed her suppliers as partners and looked to them to demonstrate a similar sense of entrepreneurialism. 'You've got to find a supplier that you can get on with and work with', she says.

She knew exactly what type of coffee blend she wanted, and her first supplier, from the London-based branch of an Italian roastery, shared her passion. The resulting concoction subsequently won numerous awards including the Best Cappucino in London (voted by *The Independent on Sunday* newspaper) and Best Espresso in London (voted by the *Guardian* newspaper). They moved onto sourcing the right food, from pastries and muffins to croissants and bagels; all to support their vision of providing the perfect coffee experience.

Hiring the right calibre of staff was a challenge in itself and again, Sahar and Bobby were looking for employees who demonstrated initiative and flair. Their first employees included two members poached from sandwich bar, Pret A Manger.

They gave themselves a year to establish the brand and opened their first outlet in London's South Molton Street in November 1995. It broke even in nine months.

'Every morning of my life started with a coffee and fat-free muffin at Coffee Republic', she recalls of the early days of the business. Her fondest moments were watching passers-by carrying a Coffee Republic cup, 'every time you saw a queue outside, every time we had a new product', she recalls.

There is often a moment when an entrepreneur feels they have truly 'made it'. For Sahar, that was in 1997 when the business floated.

'You realise', she says, 'that there's a momentum here and it's not all relying on you. We moved to an office and things moved onto a different level!'

Sahar and Bobby retained 27% of the company. At that point, they had six stores – the Coffee Republic model had steamed ahead, proving staggeringly successful. (Indeed, their growth rate of one to 100 stores in just five years saw them named by Deloitte Touche as the second fastest-growing company in the UK in 2002.)

> ## Role **MODEL**
>
> I don't like to get too focused on any one particular role model – I get inspired by many stories. I also believe that products as well as people can be role models – my role model for Skinny Candy is Green & Black's.

However, with hindsight, she admits it was a mistake giving away such a large part of the company not knowing how big it was going to be.

'We gave it away because we needed to expand quickly', she explains. They moved into proper office space and expanded their team of two to include finance, HR, property and project managers.

Despite fierce competition, by 1998, Coffee Republic had expanded to 20 stores and by the following year, they had recognised the need for someone with serious management experience and hired a managing director, with Bobby as CEO and Sahar as marketing director.

Sahar estimates that at its peak, Coffee Republic had 110 outlets, 35 full-time office and around 1,500 part-time staff. As annual turnover reached £30m but feeling that her entrepreneurial flair was no longer required, Sahar eventually stepped down from Coffee Republic in 2001. It's her one lasting regret.

'Looking back, it was a mistake to leave', she says. 'We shouldn't have left it at that stage. The problem is when you bring in managers and things change; people take on egos and you lose touch with the core of the business. I stepped aside and then you lose control. You're not pumping that passion through the company. If I were to go back, I'd have the confidence to say, "I'm getting a manager but I'm still the entrepreneur." You want a leadership role and a management role. It's good to keep your leadership role, which I didn't, which was my mistake.'

Describing the months following her departure as 'very difficult', Sahar poured her energies into writing a best-selling book, *Anyone Can Do It*. Based on her experiences with Coffee Republic, she says it's her proudest personal accomplishment.

She still has many people asking her for business advice, but says that she can't give it because she's only written from her own experiences.

'You've got to go with your own gut and see what you want to do', she advises. 'No one, not even Mr. Branson, can tell you if your idea will work.'

She has also launched her new venture, a range of sugar-free confectionery, Skinny Candy, currently stocked in Selfridges, Harvey Nichols, Holland & Barrett, Topshop, Waitrose and Coffee Republic. Sahar eventually hopes to get it into the retail multiples and across the world.

'Following the dream filled up the void', she says of Coffee Republic. 'I never used to believe in the serial entrepreneur, but it's such a buzz. Once you do it, it's something that you want to do again.'

Sahar encourages other entrepreneurs who also believe 'anyone can do it' to just go for it:

You can make whatever dream you want happen in your life. It's about being true to yourself and to your vision. The thing about setting up on your own is that you are forever responsible for every single thing that happens to you. You get very emotionally involved with any business you start, it's a tremendous responsibility. Sometimes I'll look at people on holiday and wonder how they feel – they are really on holiday! They switch off their mobiles and email for two weeks and I think, 'how could anyone possibly do that?'

In recognition of her business flair, Sahar has won an impressive array of awards. She has been named a 'Pioneer to the life of the Nation' by the Queen, one of the 100 Most Influential Women in Britain 2003 by the *Daily Mail* and one of the 20 most powerful women in Britain by *The Independent on Sunday*. She is also a speaker ambassador for the Prince's Trust. The only thing she says she feels pressured by is the whole 'having it all, leaving it too late' train of thought.

'Working mums vs. stay at home mums', she says, 'it doesn't need to be like that. I hate that and think it does a disservice to women. There is somewhere in between. The power should be given to women to structure it as they like rather than seeing it as a gender thing.'

She says her experiences with Coffee Republic have changed her irrevocably:

Advice to other
ENTREPRENEURS

Be true to yourself and your vision, and just go for it.

Originally I trained as a solicitor but I realised I wasn't very good at it; it just wasn't me. It wasn't where my talent lies. If I had stayed being a solicitor I would have been a pretty mediocre solicitor. And with entrepreneurship, I've realised you've got to go on that journey; you've got to find what you are good at because every single person is a star at one thing, and the million dollar question in life is finding where you are the star — finding that one area where you are special. That's the ultimate quest.

Would she do it all again? Absolutely. 'I still go to Coffee Republic for my latte', she says finally. 'I wouldn't go anywhere else.'

Sally Preston

Entrepreneurs need to be 'Weebles!' So says 42-year-old Sally Preston, founder of frozen babyfood and kids' food business, Babylicious.

'You need to be able to constantly bounce back from disappointment. If you think it is an easy ride from your kitchen table, that you'll see your kids and partner more often and it will all be rather jolly and you'll be very rich, then you are sadly deluded.'

Typically frank words from a woman who has faced her fair share of adversity whilst determinedly setting up a very successful business. Incorporated in 2001, Babylicious started trading in mid-2002. Since then, it has won numerous awards, including the Start-up Stars top prize in 2003, which Sally admits, was her proudest achievement. 'That was huge, not just for me but for everyone who had been involved. It was big recognition.'

Following the launch of Kiddylicious, a frozen meal range for toddlers in 2005, Sally is about to go to market with her latest venture, Snackylicious, a range of snacking products for kids.

'They're apple rings dipped in fruit juices and then dried. No additives, no salt. Less than 1% fat. They are delicious. Each bag is the equivalent of an apple, but they're crispy like crisps and they're healthy like apples and they've got no SO_2 in them; they've not been dipped in citric acid or anything like that', she says firmly.

Sally's products have made a big impact on UK supermarkets and are available at retailers including Asda, Sainsbury's, Ocado, Boots and Budgens. As a qualified food scientist, she has strong technical credentials – having worked for Marks & Spencer for 11 years – that go hand in hand with being a mum to two young children. So it's fair to assume that she knows what she's doing.

'If you can communicate to your audience that you are professionally qualified, capable and genuinely passionate about what you are doing then I believe mums trust you. If I was part of a huge corporation, they wouldn't believe the story at all', she says.

Leaving Marks & Spencer when her son Jack was a year and a half, she went into business alone, creating a new way of feeding babies and setting it up from her dining room. 'My aim was to create and make commercially available a range of products. Products I wish I, as a mum, could have bought – frozen babyfood. And that's exactly what I did.'

She freely admits that the impetus to get going was her personal life, which she says was in turmoil. She had just gone through a highly acrimonious divorce, had two young children and been diagnosed with skin cancer. On finally beginning to get her life back together, she realised that 'life is not a dress rehearsal':

I didn't want to be sitting there in 10 year's time thinking 'oh, I had that idea; I wish I'd done that.' I reached rock bottom and you do get to a place when you just think 'why not?' when so many other things are bad, what difference is it going to make?

The name 'Babylicious' was made up one Saturday evening over a bottle of wine with friends.

Sally launched Babylicious and Kiddylicious to offer a new way of eating for children

We thought, 'What is it? Well, its baby food, it's delicious, its babylicious and that will do! And it literally was as quick as that. Just round the table with a group of mates at a dinner party. And I registered it very quickly. There were no big focus groups or research – it just felt like a good name. Then when you've got the 'Licious' bit, the rest just flows from there: Kiddylicious, Snackylicious, Tastylicious. We also own Fruitylicious. You can get a bit carried away of course – you can imagine some of our sessions! I don't really get all these companies who have great big marketing budgets and research themselves up their own bottoms. Just follow your instinct! People don't like making mistakes any more (or maybe they are not allowed to) but you've got to because that's how you learn!

The initial research for Babylicious was simple: 'a couple of mates and I were chatting about baby food and what we wished we could buy at a playground backdoor. That was my market research. That's all I did.'

Sally admits to 'pathologically hating' her first business plan. Written off a floppy disc, it was a frustrating process because the programme would only allow her to put so many characters in the box:

I'm not really sure how you're meant to write a business plan that limits each section to a specific space; you spend more time editing your words down than actually writing it. It took a few weeks. I had no financial projections; my accountant at the time did some very crude cash flow forecasts but it was a bit of an amateur affair really.

Sally went to see every single high street bank to raise an initial £50,000. However all banks bar none then said it was a great idea but it was such a good idea that it should have been done before. 'Therefore', says Sally, trying to explain their rationale, 'it must be high risk because if someone else hadn't done it earlier, then there must be a reason why.' Consequently, they all offered Sally the money but with such 'enormously hideous' interest payments and penalties for non-payment that it became non-viable. So she remortgaged the house she had just bought back off her ex-husband for £50,000, and a little bit later borrowed a further £25,000 off her parents, which she has now paid back.

'Nobody', she says unequivocally, 'either family or friends, ever said to me: "you are bonkers." They might have said it behind my back but they never said it to my face, because everybody believed that the principles of giving babies better-quality food which saved mums time was absolutely in step with the way the world was going. The concept wasn't flawed, therefore no one said to me I was actually mad, and I just did it.'

The start-up process was beset with tough challenges. At the very beginning Sally was presented with a bitter trademark battle; 'someone else', (she maintains she doesn't know who) registered the name 'Babylicious' at exactly the same time as she did. So she had to change their name to Tastylicious before launching.

'I was really annoyed. I felt it had been done deliberately. It had been filed in bad faith but it took us a year to prove it. And it cost us £34,000 to go from Babylicious to Tastylicious and then back to Babylicious. That was quite challenging.'

Just as the company got going at the back end of 2002, a woman, purporting to work for the Advertising Standards Authority, said that Marks & Spencer had made an official complaint against Sally, her product and her company; 'as a consequence, people cancelled meetings, advertising and PR. It turned out to be a hoax, obviously.'

Sally received confirmation from the Advertising Standards Authority and from Marks & Spencer that there was no such issue. It took her a month to claw her way back, reinstating numerous meetings and business.

'That was really tough because you know someone is attacking you but they're hiding behind someone else's name', recalls Sally.

She accepts that everyone makes mistakes and that's how you learn.

The important thing is not to make the same one twice. You have to accept you will make them, and that as a small business, the cost of making that mistake is massive. In a large company, it gets absorbed into everything else, but in a small company, the costs are huge. You've got to prepare yourself for that.

In hindsight, there are things she would have done differently. 'I had never worked in brands or marketing and I grossly underestimated their impact; I would have paid more attention to that at an earlier stage.'

Her company guidelines are simple:

All of our food, bar none, must be made out of ingredients that are found in a kitchen. So there is nothing in our food that you wouldn't find at home. That's number one. Number two – would I feed the food to my children and would the team here give it to their children? If the answer is no, then we shouldn't be doing the product. And the third thing is do we feel good about this product and does it feel right? Is it doing something that is healthy and nutritious and is not contrived? There are just too many products now that are made up by marketing people. Our motto is 'we make it like you make it'.

Sally describes the initial start-up period as exciting and great fun, 'just like playing or being in a child's sweetshop.'

You go off, design a brand and do things; you don't have to ask anyone's permission. You just do what you want and what you believe is right. You don't have to submit it to 49 million committees, and a million and one people's opinions don't have to be taken into account. There's no politics and you get on with it and make it happen. It's remarkable, with minimal interference, how much you can achieve. Its great fun to start with but the problem is when you have to start selling it!

Babylicious doesn't disclose its financial figures, but Sally will say that 'growing' is the key phrase. Based in Ealing, West London, the company currently has a core team of 10. Believing that it's important to know your own limitations, Babylicious outsources its PR, technical support, legal, accountancy and store fulfilment work to a further six personnel.

Since those early days, Babylicious has taken in three lots of private investment, one each year since 2004 to constantly grow the business. Sally retains 30%; employees have 20% and private investors, across a group of about 30, have the remaining 50%.

'We wouldn't have survived otherwise. I would rather own 30% of a multi-million pound company than 100% of nothing. That was one of the things my mum told me very early on; "don't be greedy, let go of it for the growth of the company."' Indeed, Sally says her mum is her biggest champion, 'a real star who goes in and sorts things for me at Sainsbury's and Tesco in Sheffield. She gives them hell if it's not displayed properly.'

Her advice for a would-be entrepreneur is typically upfront:

It's incredibly hard, much harder than I had ever dreamt it would be. It takes much more money than you believe you can spend. Trust me, you can spend it! The key is to have a genuinely good idea (not an idea that your mates says is a great idea.) You have to really sense-check it. Once you've decided you do have a good idea and you're really prepared for the rough and tumble of being disappointed endlessly, then give it a go.

And would she do it all again? Probably not!

Advice to other ENTREPRENEURS

Make sure you have a genuinely good idea, be prepared for potential pitfalls, and go for it! Learn to be a Weeble!

I don't regret it; there's no point because we're here now. But have I found it hard, has it rocked me to the core on several occasions? Yes, it has. Has it taken me to levels I've found almost unbelievably low? Yes, it has. But you have to bounce back. You have to be incredibly strong.

Sally has what she describes as 'one massively unfulfilled ambition'; to ensure that frozen babyfood and frozen kids food are in every single retailer for every single mother in a place they can find it:

If I could stop the mums phoning us, emailing us and writing to us saying "why can't I get your product?", then that would be a huge achievement. It would be a lot easier if retailers could empower buyers to be more strategic and to understand what we're doing for the total feeding of babies and health. We aren't just looking at the bottom cash line every single day. We fight for what we believe in. We don't always get our point understood, but sometimes we do.

In what she regards as a David and Goliath situation, Sally is concerned that small brands in the food and drink sector may die fairly soon if the market does not fundamentally look at the way big brands dominate space, flex their massive marketing budgets and have influential power. 'Retailers need to look at the way small innovative suppliers are treated and have a more nurturing, supportive approach. There is more genuine innovation coming out of small entrepreneurial companies, but it is the larger brands who continue to dominate the retail landscape', she says.

She admits to not taking as much notice of her competitors as she should. 'But', she says, 'I take a different view on that – if someone has already done it, then we shouldn't be doing it. We're looking for that next big idea.'

Babylicious has not yet turned a profit. But Sally says she's quite relaxed about it. 'As a result we don't pay any company tax and we're quite clear that we're in a growth and brand development stage and we should re-invest everything we make into good people, new processes, innovative packaging, new marketing and exciting ideas. We don't say we want to make £100k profit this year; what we say is, we've got £100k spare, let's develop a new product.'

However, saying that, Sally does believe they are likely to turn a profit by the end of 2007. She is now looking to go overseas and has trademarked Babylicious and Kiddylicious globally. 'The concept of good-quality food without salt is one that mothers want all over the world', she says.

She doesn't network all the time, simply because she doesn't have time and would rather be at home with her children. But she doesn't mind picking up the phone and only this week picked it up to the 'lady who runs JoJo Maman Bébé' (Laura Tenison) and spoke to her because 'I can see a synergy. I don't have a problem picking up the phone and talking to people if I think there's a really mutually beneficial reason for doing it, but I wouldn't network just for the sake of a bottle of wine. I'd rather have that with my mates!'

———————— *JW* ————————

sweatyBetty

Tamara Hill-Norton

Even if you're slightly superstitious, you'd probably avoid opening your store on Friday 13th, but it proved to be auspicious for 36-year-old entrepreneur Tamara Hill-Norton, who launched her first sweatyBetty store in 1998. Almost a decade on, the women's active wear retailer has come on in leaps and bounds.

sweatyBetty currently has 24 boutiques across London and the UK, including concessions in Harrods and Selfridges and stand-alone stores in Bluewater, Cambridge and Manchester.

The company has 25 staff in its Fulham head office and around 120 in stores and turned over £8m in the year to March 2007. Describing its ethos as 'fitness with fashion' and with a strong emphasis on fun and ethics for both clients and staff, sweatyBetty stocks everything from gym and yoga clothes to bikinis and snow wear with celebrity clients including appropriately named model, 'The Body', Elle McPherson.

Having her own business was always something mother of three Tamara had considered. As part of her French and German university degree, she spent several months in Paris. She was inspired by their lingerie stores and returned to the UK to work at underwear retailer Knickerbox, determined to set up her own store.

It proved to be an excellent learning experience:

Working in Knickerbox was definitely my first encounter working in retail. It was a fascinating company to work for. I learned a lot. What I learnt not to do was the 'Head Office', where you tended to exist in your little ivory tower and you didn't really get out to the stores much – it was very much them and us. One of the manufacturers we were dealing with was actually doing sportswear at the time and I thought 'this is interesting.' It was the first time I'd seen a range designed for women specifically and so I started looking into that.

It was during her six months of research that she had a poor bra-buying experience in a high street store, which only confirmed her thoughts that the typical sportswear buying experience for women was intimidating and frustrating. When faced with a 16-year-old boy advising her on sports bra purchasing, she decided the time was absolutely right for a friendly female environment with sales girls who were passionate about the product.

With the seeds of her business idea sown, she turned to husband Simon, then at business school, to put together their first business plan. It took months. 'We put together this massive catalogue-sized business plan, and actually when we went to see everyone it was more a question of them investing in the two of us and the way we were so passionate in the idea than them reading through a really rigorous plan.'

Happily, Tamara was surprised to find that securing funding wasn't that difficult: 'I think it was about five friends we managed to get £5,000 off. We also had another investor who gave us £20,000. We had some bank debt as well.'

Then there was the issue of the name, eventually decided upon with the help of copious amounts of alcohol, brainstorming and tongues firmly in cheek.

We were trying to come across to women in a male-dominated sports world; to say we're starting up a concept that we want to be all encompassing. We don't want to be scary and although we're going to be selling lycra and

sweatyBetty focuses on fitness with fashion

things like that, we want everyone to be having a bit of it. We're not real athletes necessarily, we maybe just go to the gym once a week if that, or we just like to wear the sportswear and look good. Love it or hate it, you have that reaction to the name and people will remember it.

Feminine, irreverent, inspirational and fun, were the key brand guidelines from the start.

With the name sussed, the next challenge was getting the big sportswear brands to support them:

They just think obviously they could deliver stock and you could go bust and not pay for them. They're frightened you're going to be another discounter flogging shell-suits to kids. We had to really convince them we were going to be specialist and top end and the way we did that was to say to Nike 'Adidas are on board' and to Adidas, 'Nike are onboard'. Eventually they went with it.

They had to demonstrate that they meant business by presenting their business plans and giving certain personal guarantees – but they drew the line at putting their house up as collateral; 'I know quite a few people do end up doing that and then it's so likely that you are going to fail and that you might lose everything. We made sure we didn't risk too much at the beginning.'

Whilst Tamara's rental plans for their first shop in Notting Hill hit the inevitable delays, the stock she'd ordered began piling up at home. 'Without any stock you can't open a shop but without a shop you can't sell your stock', she says. They opened later than planned and with extra product stacked to the rafters.

'I was able to cancel some and push some back', recalls Tamara, 'but then of course because its your first thing and you've convinced all these people you are a proper business person and you're not going to be opening a rubbish concept, you can't then go and say "actually I screwed up, I haven't got a shop after all." I think I actually lost about a stone in weight.'

Friends, family and even the builders, turned up to offer their support at the official opening. 'We just wanted everyone who had helped out there. It was so much a heart-and-soul thing; my real baby.'

In the beginning, the actual day-to-day running of the business was left to Tamara. Husband Simon came on board two years later, after the birth of their first child, to support the main office.

'I managed to get a shop assistant at the beginning', she recalls, 'but after about two months she resigned so I did Christmas on my own! It was hideous but I quickly decided because I was so enjoying taking money that I would open seven days a week. So it was a bit mad for a few months!'

Running her own store meant getting her hands dirty and involving herself in every aspect of the business from opening the shop each morning and sweeping the floors, to greeting customers, calling suppliers and dealing with the stock coming in:

Now I have a really structured timetable because I'm only working three days a week so I have to get it all done. We have a more typical big-retailer style where Mondays are all about analysis on the previous weeks trading, setting up for the week, and looking through reports. Tuesdays are my production day where we sit with the designers and production development manager and thrash through, and then Wednesdays I tend to do store visits or I'll have external meetings with people. It's pretty much structured like that every week. It's a bit of a time management planning thing!

Tamara's initial plan was to plug the gaps left by other major sportswear retailers.

When I was researching, there seemed to be so many amazing brands out there that weren't being retailed in the right way. Our concept was to showcase these fantastic female sports brands that you never see, in a beautiful, friendly environment. But what we found was that no one was catering for the yoga customer or the leisure customer, the nice tracksuits and roll down pants; that type of thing. I suppose with my background being all in own-label at Knickerbox I thought 'we've got to go down that route, and we're so close to our customers we know what to do for them.'

Tamara soon realised that due to the big retailers' discounting policy, making a profit on sportswear would be very difficult. And so, confident that sweatyBetty knew its customers well enough, she decided to shift the focus of the business much more towards own-label, something she admits that she wishes they'd done earlier.

That's been quite a recent development but we've crept up to 40% own-label in the last five years. In the last year, we have gone up to 50% and we're aiming to get to 60–65% in the next couple of years. We've had to re-finance a lot as we've gone along – we haven't been profitable enough not to. One of the things we could have done is to have looked at that earlier and dealt with it earlier in terms of maybe doing more own-label or negotiating better terms with suppliers. That is all down to confidence actually. I didn't have the confidence to just go for it.

For Tamara, that confidence was boosted by having a supportive husband:

'Luckily', she says, 'it's worked well for the two of us with him being very strong on the financial side and me on the product side; it's a natural affiliation. But even if it's not your partner, I think you need someone else to be able to start up the business with you– as long as both of you are passionate about what you're doing. You need someone to bounce the ideas off when things are going wrong and to support you. If you've got your own strengths, play to those and don't cross over!'

With her Knickerbox experience still weighing on her mind, Tamara was determined to run her business differently.

At sweatyBetty we really try to make sure that we're one team together. We make sure we all get out to do store visits and have a lot of communication; otherwise, as retail staff, you can feel a bit undervalued. It's really important to feel that you're making a difference to the business as a whole.

When it comes to business, Tamara feels it's equally essential to look at things differently to men.

I'm really intrigued whenever I hear women in business talking. For me, the whole issue of women in business is how you cope with having a family and juggling that life with business. You can do just as good a job as men, if not better, but I think you can probably do that on a part-time basis because your management skills are possibly better than men and you're going to get more out of your team. You've delegated more, whereas the man has to be there five or seven days a week. I don't mind this 'women in business' tag and I think it's important for us to talk about it and for people to understand – men in particular! Women have an instinct, a feeling for where things are going.

That feminine instinct has served Tamara well. In 2001, sweatyBetty was named Sports Retailer of the Year, and in 2003, Tamara won the *Harper's and Queen* Entrepreneur of the Year award.

Describing her parents as her biggest fans, Tamara also says her eldest daughter harbours ambitions of running either Marks & Spencer or sweatyBetty when she is old enough.

Advice to other ENTREPRENEURS

Have vision, passion and focus.

Her advice to other women entrepreneurs is to be passionate about what you're doing; 'research the market and make sure you're actually going to make money out of it', she advises.

> *If you want to do it as a hobby, fantastic, but if you've got investors then they're all going to need a return on their money so you've got to make sure it's a viable proposition and that you're going to make money out of it. You've got to have vision, you've got to have your five-year plan and be focused. I think you've got to listen to other people when they say 'maybe try this' and take it on board but know where you are going – and you can lead everyone from that point.*

When it comes to leading her own team, Tamara sheepishly admits she knows she is still far too hands on:

> *Every entrepreneur is a bit like that and in fact, it's perhaps the downfall of entrepreneurs! I'm aiming to be a proper director so actually I'm not having to make the day-to-day decisions, which can help. I can go off on holiday for two weeks and it's absolutely fine; no-one will contact me. Everyone has their own responsibilities but I just can't help it, I love getting involved in little nitty-gritty detail on product.*

Looking ahead, Tamara wants to move the sweatyBetty own-label brand forward.

> *This last year, I feel like it has been my biggest challenge ever, although of course I've forgotten what it was like right from the beginning... I want to take a bit more of a step back and be more of a creative director. We want to be opening more stores, becoming more profitable and growing our website. That would be the ultimate!*

Vanessa Knox-Brien and Baukjen de Swaan Arons-van Sonsbeeck

It was fate and a shared passion for fashion that brought Vanessa Knox-Brien and Baukjen de Swaan Arons van Sonsbeeck together by the swimming pool at plush Babington House. Both were on 'babymoon' with their partners and heavily pregnant.

'She was wearing these fabulous Prada sandals', says Baukjen. 'My husband told me to go and speak to her and I did. I liked her immediately. And luckily it was a two-way street.'

New-Yorker Vanessa and Amsterdam-born Baukjen are the brains behind Isabella Oliver, the e-tailer and mail-order maternity brand they set up together in 2003.

'We were both in the same position', recalls Baukjen. 'We had great careers, were pregnant and wondering what to do.'

'I was a designer, had just relocated from New York', continues Vanessa, 'and was struggling to find something to do – but I didn't want to start a lingerie company on my own in the UK. I never wanted to feel bad about how I looked and made sure I had a wardrobe of things to feel good in. People on the street stopped me when I was pregnant to ask me where I got my clothes. I didn't shop maternity – everyone was embarrassed to be in those shops but had no choice. I thought maybe we had something here.'

Baukjen was the international brand manager for Orange, and Vanessa, as a head designer for top US lingerie company, Victoria's Secret, had impressive fashion and design credentials. The two women realised they had complementary skill sets and decided to set up in business together.

'The penny dropped that maybe this was a good balance', says Baukjen. 'Geoff, my husband (a former CFO at Heinken and Shell) joined in on the financial side and completed the pie.'

It is an enviable pie, with clients including Trinny Woodall (who famously ordered the entire Isabella Oliver collection whilst pregnant), Anna Friel, Myleene Klass and Marcia Cross from *Desperate Housewives*, as well as an impressive celebrity following in the USA, where the clothes regularly feature in *US Weekly* and *People* magazine. Operating out of warehouse offices in London's Kentish Town, Isabella Oliver, named after their children, has a staff of 25 and turnover of £5m.

From the beginning, their mission was clear: 'to give pregnant women clothes that are stylish, sexy and versatile', says Vanessa. Each business partner (Vanessa, Geoff and Baukjen) invested around £70,000 to fund the growth of the company. They also secured a £180,000 loan from the DTI, 'although', says Vanessa, 'their money came later and we had to keep on going and hoping. But in the meantime we couldn't lose time, so we kept putting up our own money and kept ploughing ahead to meet our launch.'

They spent months putting together an extensive business plan. 'One bank were very enthusiastic but said no at the end. Fortunately, another went with us from the word "go"', recalls Baukjen.

Their market research was based on personal experience. 'We were both pregnant and couldn't find a middle-market brand that was catering to people like us', recalls Baukjen. 'Vanessa designed around 50 different styles, we did focus groups with style-conscious pregnant women and asked them which designs they would buy and why, if money wasn't an issue. We had great feedback. Vanessa is a size 8 and I am a size 14 – so we got different sides of the spectrum.'

Isabella Oliver clients include Myleene Klass and Trinny Woodall

In order to get going on their corporate image, photography and catalogue, they relied on the goodwill and favour of talented family members who coincidently specialised in those areas.

'What were the chances of all those people getting along and having the same sensibility and point of view and it really working?' recalls Vanessa. 'All these creatives and personalities came together and everyone was so excited about the brand. We started in Baukjen's front room until we were really bursting at the seams. We were packing and wrapping, taking phone calls, writing invoices and printing them. We did it all ourselves.'

Whilst they made just under £1,000,000 in their first year, they agree that their biggest challenge in setting up was still money and getting factories to work with them before they had any customers.

'The factory picked us, it wasn't vice versa', recalls Vanessa. 'When you are new, you don't have much choice. We were nobody. We had no reputation. It is a risky thing for factories to get involved with a company and do product development knowing that it may not lead anywhere, because most companies don't even launch.'

'We needed to be smart and focused and we couldn't afford to do 1,000 pieces per style when we started out. There was one factory that was willing to take a chance on us. Now we have the luxury of having a choice of who we work with', recalls Baukjen.

Inspired by their idol Donna Karan ('we just adore her philosophy' says Vanessa), Isabella Oliver is all about classic and timeless pieces and fitting women of different shapes and sizes.

'We're not competing with trendy, high street stuff', say Vanessa and Baukjen. 'When you buy maternity wear, women don't want to buy a lot. They want to buy clothes that last them through. You don't want to have identifiable clothes with a print or embroidery as its great when you can create lots of different looks from one dress with different accessories.' Adds Vanessa:

It really kills me when I hear a woman say that she loved our clothes, passed them onto her sister and that they have lasted five pregnancies! I'd prefer it if all those women bought their own clothes, but if ours have lasted five pregnancies then we're very proud. We use good-quality fabrics, and that costs money but we're very well priced for what we provide.

'Vanessa and I are very much about the product and the message', says Baukjen, 'which is wonderful because those are the areas we love to be involved in.'

Geoff takes care of the operations and financial structure whilst Baukjen focuses on brand and product management and Vanessa on the design of the collection. 'Together we're much stronger than one of us', they say.

Of having a close partnership with Baukjen, Vanessa is nonplussed. 'I've always worked with women', she says:

A lot of the time, fashion is male-dominated but I've always worked for or with women and I'm a girl's girl. I don't find it strange at all, though it is very emotional at times. But that's OK; that's the way it is! We have sensitivity which is not always a good thing. Sometimes I wish I could be more of a man, not worry so much and detach myself.

Remaining honest with their customers is key at Isabella Oliver. 'Everything we launch, we believe in', says Baukjen:

I know this should always be a given, but I don't think it actually is. I don't think there are many companies who wear their clothes. We have never hidden the fact that we are the people behind the company but over the years, it's become apparent that women like to hear more about us – what we wore during our own pregnancies and how we wore it. So more and more we are including the personal touches.

These personal touches include regularly updating the Isabella Oliver blog and newsletters. The morning I had spoken to them, they had spent half an hour hand-signing 250 letters to inform favoured customers about the new brochure and asking them to spread the word, offering them 10% off their next order as an incentive.

'We are personally connected to the product. We know what women are going through', says Vanessa.

> ## *Role* **MODEL**
>
> Vanessa: Donna Karan.
> Baukjen: My mother, Anita Roddick and Natalie Massenet (Net-a-porter.)

They've quickly realised that working in maternity can be a frustrating experience. 'We're not like The White Company where people like the experience and continue to shop for four or five years', says Baukjen. 'We always have to make a first impression again and again and again. That puts a lot of pressure on the bottom line in terms of advertising. People are continually leaving us. It's a bit like a ferry – people get on, then they get off. That's something we face all the time. Thankfully, we are financially healthy, but it is a difficult market.'

They both have full-time help for their brood of children (Vanessa has two; Baukjen three). 'Without consciously knowing it, we have both chosen nannies who are extremely loving', says Baukjen. 'It's guilt!' says Vanessa. 'No one is judging me. It's *me* who puts the guilt on me. It's very admirable and noble for mums to stay at home and I know it's about personal choice, but it's much harder for me to be at home than to be here!'

Baukjen has strong opinions when it comes to perceptions and expectations of working women. 'I don't see why it's such a big deal', she argues. 'You go to school, you do your GCSEs, A-levels and there was no question that I would also go to university. So society is training people up, but five or six years later, you're expected to feel guilty to continue on the path that you were on. I just don't get that. I think that women should have the choice and if they do choose to stay at home, wonderful; I think my children would prefer it if I did. But I also hope that when my kids are 20, they will know a mother who is a happy, fulfilled being. I might not be the whole 'cookie' mummy but I'm another kind of mummy and there's no less love and there's no less interest.'

'My husband hates me when I'm not working', laughs Vanessa, when considering how she reconciles being a mother and businesswoman. 'This is something I need to do to be a happy person and a good mother; to explore my own life and realise my own talents. I don't want to transfer disappointment onto my own kids, especially a daughter. I want her to see that you work and contribute and if you have a dream, you go for it. It makes me a better mother.'

They both believe that passion is a characteristic shared by all entrepreneurs. And for those looking to launch their own companies, they strongly warn against underestimating the time involved. Says Baukjen:

It's not about whether you love the idea, but whether the customers you have in mind love the idea. A lot of people miss that. Also think about what you're not great at and think about where you can get that from. And do everything as cheaply as you possibly can. Don't overload yourself with overhead before you can afford it.

Advice to other
ENTREPRENEURS

Do something you believe in and ensure it makes financial sense.

'Do something you really believe in', encourages Vanessa to other would-be entrepreneurs. 'Mothers are really great inventors and designers. Do your research and have tons of support; be aware that it is going to be a sacrifice.'

'Have a concept that makes financial sense', adds Baukjen. 'Just because you have a nice idea and great designs, it doesn't necessarily mean it will translate into business and turnover and margins.'

'You're not good until you are selling and making money', says Vanessa.

Making the one million pound mark and changing their initial postal pick up from a small truck to a huge 18-wheeler were also landmark moments for the company. Then, in November 2006, Isabella Oliver was a finalist for the *Drapers* Awards 'e-tailer of the year'.

'That we were even acknowledged by that organisation, and the high street and our peers, was great', they agree. They were also listed as one of the top 50 companies to watch by a business magazine and awarded Best Transactional Website in Europe by ECMOD. 'Although', says Baukjen, 'our business isn't really driven on awards. It's driven on word of mouth.'

They are constantly looking to improve their customer service. 'We could really do better than we're doing just by tailoring our emails to the various climate zones', says Vanessa of their customers in Australia and New Zealand. 'We have a lot to do – we've just scratched the surface.'

They launched in the US in August 2005 and admit they have 'tons of work to do' to improve on it there. They're also keen on exploring partnerships with big companies and Baukjen confesses that she 'would love to see Isabella Oliver for Debenhams or Isabella Oliver designing for Top Shop. That would be wonderful.'

Motivation to keep going is not an issue. 'It's not a hobby. This is hard work. I like financial independence, being successful and doing something

I love to do, so it's a win–win', says Vanessa. 'It's a no-brainer. It's our company and that's motivation enough.'

'It's not needed', agrees Baukjen. 'I'm so excited every day. Life couldn't be better really.'

OUT SEC

Vanessa Phillips

Whoever says secretarial courses aren't productive should have a chat with Vanessa Phillips. The Irish mother of three has tap-tapped her way to success with internet secretarial company, OutSec.co.uk.

The company provides online digital transcription and was set up in 2002. Projected turnover for 2007/2008 is between £1.25m and £1.5m.

Operating out of offices in Stradsett, Norfolk, OutSec has a core team of six staff and a database of over 300 secretaries. Vanessa herself estimates she's between 70 and 80 words per minute. 'I talk too fast for my own good and therefore will practically trip over myself in typing!' she laughs.

Vanessa initially set up the business on her own until her husband Richard joined her a year later as operations and IT development director.

She'd been working for a merchant bank in London as a PA and then with a colleague started up the London College of Finance; an experience she found exciting and challenging. However, following her marriage and a move to the country, she reverted to PA audio typing whilst bringing up her twin sons, Toby and Hugo, and her daughter Emma with the intention of 'setting up a business when the children were more manageable in their teens!' However all this came sooner than anticipated and whilst the children were still not old enough for full-time school, she discovered her own gap in the market. Not one to wait, she quickly began researching the market and established that no one was providing online digital transcription – mainly because the connection speeds to the internet at that time were too slow.

Intrigued, Vanessa soon realised it was 'an opportunity not to be missed. It just seemed rude not to! I tested out the equipment and looked into potential national and then international staff recruitment.' And she adds that 'being my own boss was heaven!'

With the price of digital recorders plummeting and the spread of BT broadband increasing, the potential market for OutSec seemed huge. 'Now any company can have access to their own British typist at the click of a mouse and OutSec is going to be the company that provides that service', says Vanessa.

She borrowed £15,000 against an endowment policy to get the business going, prepared a business plan and approached a highstreet bank for a loan. But she says that 'in the end we did not need it. We were in profit from day one – mainly, of course, since I did all of the typing. I put in all the hours that I could; I then recruited locally and got a network of typists going. Clients started coming to us by word-of-mouth but since all work came through me by means of email it was only a matter of time before it was not humanly possible to cope with the volumes.'

All that profit, however, was poured back into the fledgling business and invested in a unique web-based system called FileManager which was developed in-house. Vanessa says this has been one of the main USP's in her business.

'It is evolving all of the time and now provides a workflow solution that clients are finding very attractive', she says. Those clients are mainly drawn from the financial, medical, legal and property sectors and include many household names.

A self-confessed multi-tasker, initially Vanessa tried to do everything herself. 'Not only to save money', she explains, 'but also because it is essential that the managing director understands the grass roots of the

Vanessa and her team are passionate about enabling women to combine work and home life

company. I don't take people's word for it; I fully evaluate everything myself.'

In the early days of the business, she did get support from friends, but admits getting them to empathise was sometimes tough: 'during the first three years I would not have been able to take time out for a funeral – literally. This would never have been understood by my family and friends who are not in business.'

One of her biggest challenges was actually selling the concept of online transcription to a sceptical and uncertain target audience:

Before BT began rolling out broadband to a wider audience, outsourcing the typing of 'large' digital sound files wasn't possible. Also, people's perceptions were that the quality would not be as good as in-house support. However our huge database of global typist applications enables us to choose the crème de la crème, whereas companies recruiting locally have a limited number of quality staff to choose from. This gives us the opportunity to supply our clients with a superior quality online facility and deliver a three-way saving in wages, employment and space.

Clients dictate their work and send it to OutSec via the FileManager programme which is fully compatible with most company operating systems. 'FileManager also encompasses automatic email receipt mechanisms combined with automated invoices for both client and typist', says Vanessa.

The other challenge she faced was more personal – the old adage of work–life balance and not being able to devote as much attention to her children as she'd like. 'But then life's not ideal for a great many people and I am very lucky to have such an exciting opportunity come my way', she reasons.

Vanessa admits that it's never easy reconciling being a businesswoman and a mother but ultimately, she's doing it all for her family's overall benefit.

'It's a constant battle to try and do one's best for the children with the realisation that the business provides finance for the family and is of equal importance. OutSec is my fourth child in many ways, in that it is constantly challenging for my affections!' she says.

Despite the obstacles, she is adamant that there was never a time that she felt like quitting. 'No way!' she exclaims.

I am a Virgo and a sticker! Some people would call it stubbornness, although I rather feel that it is more than this. I won't stick to something if it doesn't make sense. I am also a realist and know when it is best to leave something alone. I think I have a balanced outlook and only remain 'stubborn' when it is feasible and sensible to do so! I don't, however, give up easily; choosing to go down each and every avenue to ensure that I have covered every possibility. If, at the end of that, I decide that something is just not possible it is only then that I will walk away from it. But I do feel that any knowledge gathered in the process will provide me with more ammunition for the next fight!

To date, OutSec have won an impressive number of regional and e-commerce awards, including Investor In People Accreditation in March 2005, the DTI E-Commerce Regional Award for Teleworking in 2004 and

2005 and a Best Expansion Plan and Best Business Plan Award in 2005. In 2006 Vanessa was selected as an Entrepreneur of The Year winner as well as being one of four finalists in The European Women of the Year 2006 Awards.

Role **MODEL**

Peter Mulhall of Business Link Norfolk who advises us and is second-to-none!

'Think carefully about what it is that you are doing', she says to other would-be entrepreneurs, 'and the people who will be directly affected by it. Consider whether you will be able to cope with having to compartmentalise so many different areas of your life. If, on balance, you still feel a burning desire to do it then go for it! The worst thing is to regret not doing something. It is better to have tried and failed than not try at all. We only have one life so make the most of it!'

Vanessa believes setting up on her own has given her the freedom to realise that you can do anything you want to, if you want to do it badly enough. 'The restrictions', she says, 'are that there are only so many hours in the day to do them!'

She could, she says, never return to work for someone else. She is keen for OutSec to expand, though it has been doubling in size every nine months since inception. Whilst initially having her own business was about the money, 'now', she says, 'I just want to push the company forward to enable more women to be able to combine home commitments with work.'

To date, OutSec provides online secretarial support to more than 3,000 dictators in over 250 firms every day, 95% of whom are in the UK. The typists come from a global base of more than 300 with 5% in the USA, 5% across Australasia, 15% in Europe and the remaining 75% located in the UK.

When it comes to dealing with clients successfully, Vanessa has this advice:

Don't ever promise something you can't deliver and try to exceed client expectations at all times. Know your limitations and if you think it is better to turn a client away then do so; suggest an alternative as this will reap dividends. My three mottos are 'to thine own self be true', 'honesty is the best policy' and 'treat others as you would like to be treated.' I don't see that one needs to do anything much else in life to feel one has done one's best.

Vanessa's proudest achievement is reading the letters received from within her global typing pool.

'Girls around the world write personally to express their thanks for the opportunity to work from home', she says. 'Receiving awards is very exciting but not as personally important to me as some of the letters that I have received.

Motivating herself each morning is never an issue. 'It's easy', she says. 'I see the team in the office and know I have a responsibility towards them, to my family and to OutSec members and clients around the world.'

Running a technology-based business makes for constant challenges and changes. But to Vanessa, this is just what makes it so enthralling.

The world is more exciting now on the technology front than it has been since the invention of the television and radio. Radical changes in the way we work, travel and function in our lives are all being altered by technology. It is virtually a super power and it is living amongst us so, as they say, if you can't beat 'em, join 'em! and that is what I intend to do. I can't get enough of it – actually I just wish that brilliant programme Tomorrow's World was still on television. Why isn't it? This time was made for it!

When considering whether, with the awards and the million pound turnover, there has ever been a definitive moment when she felt she'd 'arrived', Vanessa shakes her head.

'No, one can ever think like that. I think I would be lost if I thought I had made it. I have far too many other ideas spinning round my head. I have only just begun!' But she is proud of getting to where she is today and does put herself firmly in the 'entrepreneurial' category:

Mainly because I only did what we used to call 'O' levels and left school at 16 so I just know that I haven't had the education that some people have had. That must mean that I use something else outside of education to make my decisions. I believe in gut feelings very strongly and luckily it's not often that I find I am at a crossroads as to a decision. Having said that I involve all of my staff in the decision-making process so it would be wrong of me to say I make all of the decisions – I don't! – we, as a team, make them and I am always reminded of the famous quote by Jack Nichols; 'every person I work with knows something better than me. My job is to listen long enough to find it and use it.'

OutSec is a meeting of a number of personalities with a common goal and a desire to change the working world for the better.

Vanessa believes OutSec heralds a new smart way for businesses to operate in the UK.

OutSec is innovative and technologically advanced and will help Britain to maintain its position in the global economy. The awards received for our technology, marketing and expansion plans alongside our Investors In People accreditation are a stamp of approval by experts in our field. We feel that we are now equipped with sufficient knowledge and expertise gained over the last five years to grow our business globally into a recognised business name.

Brave words for a brave new world of working. Just don't ask her to make you a coffee.

Advice to other ENTREPRENEURS

Don't forget that no dream is impossible, but the degree of success will be determined by market conditions, so do your research thoroughly. If both the dream and your research tell you the time is right, just go for it.

Louise Barnes

I'm proud of the fact that they gave me the most precious thing they have had apart from their children', says Louise Barnes, chief executive of active lifestyle clothing brand Fat Face.

The 42-year-old mother of three joined the Hampshire-based company as CEO in 2003, invited by company founders and self-confessed ski-bums Jules Leaver and Tim Slade. They had been impressed by her retail pedigree (Etam, the Burton Group and, more recently, brand director at Monsoon).

She also shares their philosophy that 'life is out there for those who know where to find it – be that up mountains, on waves, on skis – everywhere, in fact, except the office.'

Fat Face is named after Le Face, an Olympic black run in the French ski resort of Val d'Isere. It currently has 1400 staff and over 128 stores across the UK and Ireland. There are a further six stores abroad, four of which are franchises.

Fat Face is renowned for its casual wear, footwear and jewellery for both the active and extreme-sport lifestyles.

'They did it as they went along', says Louise, explaining how Jules and Tim funded the business. 'One was in advertising and one was a policeman working for the Met, and they used to spend their winters skiing and summers trying to surf. They came up with this idea of making some t-shirts and started Fat Face by going to the Alps and selling t-shirts out of a rucksack, door to door to all the chalets.' After doing several seasons, they had enough money to return to Fulham and open their first store in 1993.

'They had receipts from everyone that had bought t-shirts over the years and they sorted them into piles. Most of the postcodes were round the SW6 area. Quite a smart locational strategy! They gave up their jobs and invested what they had in doing that', says Louise.

She admits that despite her retail background, she hadn't heard of Fat Face before she came on board:

> I suppose I wasn't part of the Fat Face club in the way that some people are. I went along to have a look at their shops and could see, as a retailer, that there was an awful lot to be done in terms of practicalities but that the brand and staff they had were fantastic. I saw a huge opportunity.

Whilst the product and retail proposition at the time needed a lot of work, she was excited about the 'fantastic raw ingredients' she'd have to play with in driving the company forward.

'The boys were making the kind of stuff that they liked to wear', she explains. 'The womenswear wasn't terribly sophisticated. There was a lot to do on fit and fabrics and introducing different elements into the range, expanding it and updating it.'

Before she could move forward, Louise's initial job was to profile the Fat Face customer:

> We came up with three male customer types, one of whom reflected what the founders wanted: people who'd do anything for their sport. But our biggest customer was the one that I recognised, that I could see amongst my friends; the City types who still liked to go off on a skiing holiday but certainly weren't

Fat Face advocate a passion for life outside of the office

as relentless as the founders. These guys wanted something that looked a bit cool, that felt great, was comfortable and that no one was going to laugh at them in, in the pub. Once we started targeting the range towards this big pool of customers, things really took off.

Fat Face may not have been Louise's original 'baby', but that hasn't dampened her passion or enthusiasm for the business:

It feels like mine even if I didn't do the grubbing around from 1988 to 1993! It's a very easy business to form an emotional bond with and when you're from a product, brand and marketing background, that's how you relate to a business – as well as seeing the commercial opportunities. It doesn't really matter to me that I didn't start it because I've done the biggest part of the growth in developing the brand so it feels like mine even if it isn't really.

Louise admires Jules and Tim for having the 'humility' and gumption to admit they'd taken the business as far as they could and needed to hire someone with her experience. She says:

I know there's an awful lot of founders that never get to that point. It may have been slightly easier for the boys because what they wanted to do was go back to enjoying their life and they suddenly looked around and thought 'God, here's a big business, we never realised it would get like this, there's a load of management stuff and actually we're not very good at it, we don't want to do it, let's try and find someone who is good.'

'I think what they wanted to do', she continues, 'was build a brand and build a legacy and they realised they couldn't do it themselves. I think it's very hard for a lot of people and I'm not sure I could do it myself; if I started a business, to suddenly think "hang on someone can do this better than me." It must be an incredibly big leap to make and all credit to them. They said "we'll let you do stuff as soon as you seem comfortable with it" and three months in I was off and they let me do it, and that's the most important thing.'

What Louise brought to the business in 2003 and what she brings now are quite different. When she first joined Fat Face, turnover was about £30m, a figure she describes as 'pretty slow' compared to her previous experience at Monsoon. Initially she was 'fixing the product, fixing the management structure and using everything I knew about where were the right locations to open shops as well as my expertise as a retailer, to improve what we were doing in the stores. It was all very operational and definitely a fix-it mode.'

Louise now views her role as more strategic; her current goal is to turn Fat Face into a global brand.

> *I've been through two private equity buyouts and learnt a lot about corporate finance that I didn't know before. As our team are growing and becoming more developed, my role is one step back from the coal-face. It's about developing the right people and maintaining the Fat Face culture, making sure we protect our most important asset, which is the brand.*

The most recent buyout was by retail investor Bridgepoint, in May 2007. It purchased Fat Face from equity group Advent for an undisclosed sum. Whilst Jules and Tim haven't been involved since 2004, they retain a small stake in the business. 'That was a shrewd investment decision!' says Louise.

No slouch herself in the business acumen department, she admits her approach to the brand was necessarily different. 'How did I make the brand feel the same as when it was run by two guys who wandered around with no shoes on and board shorts?' she asks aloud.

> *I'm not like that but what they had was the magic fairy dust and this fantastic culture where everything felt inclusive so that everyone who worked there was passionate about the business, the customers were passionate about the business and they communicated to people in a very local, natural way. We've gone through a process called brand spirit where we've articulated what Fat Face means. We have these things called 'brand goggles' and for every decision made we look through our brand goggles and say 'is that right for our brand heritage, for our brand future?' and its been extremely worthwhile. I couldn't do it by gut instinct because I'm not the founders so I had to turn it into something tangible.*

When comparing women who found start-up businesses with those taking over one already established, Louise believes her advantage was the experience gained elsewhere where she 'learned it all.'

'Some people run their business intuitively and that works for as long as they want it to. Turnover was £30m for the year end of 2003/20004 – and for the year we've just gone through it was £111m. That's a huge growth curve and I don't think you could have done that so quickly if you hadn't gone through that experience of doing the jigsaw puzzle before', she says.

The fresh eyes thing is always good and there's some things that the founders believed were incredibly important to the business that I agree with and there are others I think they gave the wrong focus to. It does help when you look at things in a slightly less emotive way. There are some tough decisions to be made where you're growing a business that can be hard – particularly when there are some people who helped you right from the beginning. Sometimes the business outgrows people and I think those 'people' decisions are the ones that our founders found particularly difficult to make.

Louise is justifiably proud of what she's achieved in such a relatively short time. 'I've worked extremely hard, built a very good team and I'm very pleased with what I've done', she says. And being a woman hasn't made any difference to how she approaches the business; 'I've got a head, two arms and two legs. If I'm good enough I believe I'm going to be successful', she says.

If success is measured by awards alone, she hasn't done too badly. Fat Face was ranked number 14 in *The Sunday Times* Buyout Track 2006 and awarded the Profit Track 100 – Best Management Team 2006. Louise personally was ranked number 51 in the *Drapers* Top 100 biggest players in High Street Fashion.

To keep in touch with the Fat Face consumer, the company sponsors so-called Team Riders, individuals like Jules and Tim that have a passion for their sport. The riders include athletes, mountain bikers and international sailing crews. 'But actually we're not a business of extreme sports so it's not necessarily keeping up with these teenagers hanging upside down on a kiteboard!' says Louise. 'These customers are people like us who want to have an active approach to life. It's what we call an active mindset rather than being an extreme sports person so that activity can be walking your dog, taking your kids to Center Parcs or riding a bike. Fat Face isn't hard. It's all about your attitude.'

She credits the ability to reach such goals to the support she receives from her husband:

> I won't say it's easy having three small children while doing this job; it's not necessarily about me being 'superwoman'. It's about the support I've got at home. Particularly when you're in a private equity business, you know you've got a very short time to make an impact. What I do try and do is keep the weekend's daytime for my family and if I need to work at the weekend I say 'I need to do a bit of work, how about this time, or this time' and we'll work through it. I try to make it not impact on my family but there are times when I've had to work all weekend. I think people can feel guilty about it but I think you make choices. I'm doing this because I want to and for as long as I can explain that to my family and get their support.

Louise thinks most women have a naturally more nurturing style, an important asset in developing a business.

'I've certainly found that has helped with me. I've grown a lot of teams. It doesn't mean there aren't any men who can do it but I think nurturing, emotional intelligence and communication, in a very general sense, come to women more easily', she says.

Whilst busy working on a pre-existing brand, Louise admits she's never been tempted to start up on her own. 'I think that's much too difficult!' she says frankly. 'What I've always done is in the later running of the company. A lot of people ask me how I've done what I've done and that seems to me to be fairly easy because that's what I'm good at. Entrepreneurs have contacted me saying "how did you do this?" when I'm looking at them thinking "I could never have done what you've done!"'

Ultimately, Louise wants to transform Fat Face into a global brand; 'we've ticked the box for "are you a successful UK retailer?" We've opened in the Middle East and are opening in Singapore and Malaysia in September and we're on a real international mission', she says.

Advice to other ENTREPRENEURS

Don't be afraid to ask for help!

Fat Face has a wholesale agreement with department chain John Lewis to go into 15 of their stores by March 2008 and they're also opening their first lifestyle store in Exeter in September 2007. 'Hopefully it will set us apart. It's a lifestyle store not a big store with clothes in' says Louise.

Louise advises any woman about to take on a brand to be confident in asking for help, saying that 'people are surprisingly keen to give you advice and have a chat with you. You learn a lot from that, and at the risk of making a sweeping generalisation, I think it's a bit like asking for directions – women are a bit more likely to do it!'

CAFÉDIRECT®

Penny Newman

'**I didn't want the concept** of Cafédirect to fail', says Penny Newman of her reason for joining the UK's largest Fairtrade hot drinks company in 1998.

Promoted to managing director in 1999 and made CEO after a 2004 share issue, the 51-year-old has a consistent work record of balancing commercial and ethical trading, having spent six years with The Body Shop. She has also worked for well-known brands including Wella, Avon and Fabergé.

Cafédirect works in partnership with 37 producer organisations in 12 countries to ensure over a quarter of a million small-scale growers receive a fair price for products, thus enabling them to make a decent living. Cafédirect buys coffee from Peru, Nicaragua, Costa Rica, Mexico, Uganda, Tanzania, Rwanda, Cameroon and Haiti; tea from Tanzania,

Uganda, Kenya and Sri Lanka, and cocoa from the Dominican Republic and Cameroon.

The company sells its three major brands, Cafédirect, Teadirect and Cocodirect, through major supermarket retailers, independent retailers, Oxfam stores and Cafédirect's own online shop.

'I was just leaving The Body Shop', Penny recalls, 'and had been involved in looking at community trade, a "trade not aid" programme that was similar to Fairtrade. I was therefore asked to take a look at Cafédirect and take it forward. I was just inspired by what Cafédirect was doing, and very concerned that it needed to have more of a marketing focus. I hoped that I could use my skills and my knowledge to take it further.'

The first Fairtrade label, Max Havelaar, was launched in the Netherlands in 1989 to raise awareness of the plight of indigenous coffee farmers in Mexico.

'It was very much about the philosophy of bringing a fairer trading system to commodities and especially to coffee', says Penny, who explains that the collapse of the International Coffee Agreement in 1989 and the subsequent fall in coffee prices was the catalyst for the formation of Cafédirect.

It was set up in 1991 by four NGOs (non-governmental organisations), Oxfam Trading, Traidcraft, Equal Exchange and Twin Trading, and produced the first coffee to carry a Fairtrade mark. Cafédirect also has its own 'Gold Standard', its guarantee to pay above world market prices and support growers through tailor-made business programmes.

'The four charity organisations each put in a small amount of money, £32,500 each, to form Cafédirect Ltd. The idea came from coffee growers in Costa Rica, Mexico and Peru', explains Penny.

Describing Cafédirect as a much smaller-scale business than Body Shop, Penny compares her two experiences:

At The Body Shop I was an employee, but I wasn't leading it. The buck didn't stop with me, whereas it certainly stops with me at Cafédirect. When I joined Cafédirect there were only four people. There were many more at The Body Shop and my experience there was just to get on with it. I think my first week here I had problems with my computer; I picked up the phone to call the IT department for help then realised there wasn't an IT department at Cafédirect – I had to set up the whole thing. A lot of people who start businesses and grow them have a lot of the same experiences; you just have to roll up your sleeves

Cafédirect works with producer organisations in 12 countries

and get on with it. Some thrive on that because you're experiencing so many different things. When you're working in a big organisation, you focus on one aspect of the business, whereas here I focus on all aspects of the business.

Penny's initial focus was to get Cafédirect's coffee on supermarket shelves and raise consumer awareness about the company and its products.

'When we set ourselves up we didn't know where Fairtrade was going. It was a philosophy; there was no standard', she explains. She was however, determined to change that and establish some guiding principles:

These have evolved over time, crafted by all of us to refer to what Cafédirect stands for and what it means across the business. One of them was always to pay a fair price. The spirit, the real spirit of these principles is 'how can we always go beyond the Fairtrade concept? How can we really always ensure growers' needs and aspirations are at the heart of this company?' and also 'how do we create a simplified trading system between growers and consumers and by simplifying it, create greater value for the growers?'

In comparing the differences between women who start up their own businesses and those like herself who have assumed responsibility for another, Penny thinks its all about timing. She says:

It depends on when you take over and how long the founder has been in the business. On my experience there were four founders, not just one, and of course I took over at quite an early stage. Now a lot of people believe I was the founder of Cafédirect and I always have to correct them. I've been here too long then!

She's sensitive enough to realise that it's a two-way street and that bringing in someone externally can also be a challenge for the original architect of any business.

I think if you come in at a declining point, its easier to think maybe we need to change things. If you're still in a growth cycle, then that might be harder. Do you want to change things, or do you believe that change is needed? The new people who take over, how do they work with the founder? And is the founder in the background or the front, leading the way? I feel for both in that situation. I would think it's better for a founder not to be in the wings. Then you have the autonomy and spirit to take it on rather than thinking you are still in their shadow.

Cafédirect started making a profit from 1994. A large proportion is reinvested into tailor-made support programmes for the growers, and whilst the figure averages around 60%, Penny is keen to stress that the final sum is always dependent on growers' specific needs. Cafédirect is therefore in constant contact with its grower partners and regularly reviewing their progress and requirements.

'We can assess what is needed year by year', says Penny. 'Of course things change; like a couple of years ago the hurricane that hit our Latin American grower partners. There were some immediate needs to be addressed so we redirected money and tried to give immediate support.

We need to hear their concerns, the good bits as well as the bad. We need to be in contact with them just to be able to judge things and communicate and share things. It's not like a top looking down. I would say it's more of a two-way communication and understanding. Our grower partners are always interested to know what's going on in the market in the UK.'

The projects they focus on are varied, from supporting investments in growing better-quality coffee or tea and implementing different standards, to helping growers market their crops to local markets as well as Cafédirect.

Penny believes in moving forward, never looking back with regrets:

My view is always to learn from your mistakes and ensure that they help you in the future. I wouldn't just sit there and say 'I wish I'd done that differently' I would say 'OK, I did it wrong but I know why I made that decision or that action, hopefully next time when I have to face a similar decision, I'll bear that in mind.' I think 'regrets' is a heavy word and I try and look at things in a more optimistic way. I try to see it as my development and the development of the team. I try and share what I've got, I'm quite honest with people and I'll tell people when I've got it wrong. When we did our public share issue I was talking to our head of marketing and she was saying 'oh what do I need to do for the prospectus?' and I said 'I don't know, I've never done this before. We'll find out between us.' I think you have to take that sort of thought process. I think it's a very lonely life leading a company and you just have to put things into perspective.

She's also frank when discussing what it's meant for her being a woman in business:

I don't think it is an advantage or a disadvantage either way. I just get on and do it. I think one of the things us women can do is juggle more. I do think the

---

Role MODEL

Keep your eyes and ears open to mentoring opportunities all around you. Sometimes it's a lonely life, so it's good if you can have a situation with somebody where you can be quite open, gain advice from them, and ask them some questions that maybe you can't really do inside your own business.

sort of business Cafédirect is, you're trying to balance making lives better and making profit. It really is a juggling art and I can see and understand those dimensions and juggle those. Some people I know just cannot deal with more than one thing at a time. I think it's getting the appropriate person to do the appropriate job. Getting that match is a real art and it doesn't matter what the gender is, it's getting the right person; fitting the skills, enthusiasm and passion with the right type of job. But there are some positions where you don't need the enthusiasm and the passion and hence you need a different approach. That's the really important thing.

She was recently involved in the government's women's enterprise panel, discussing how to encourage more women into business. She discovered that the two main issues holding women back were finance and lack of self-confidence:

Maybe one of our particular traits as women is that we have self-doubt in larger chunks than men. Obviously some things you win and some things you lose. I'd still rather go to my grave knowing that I've had a go at it, rather than feeling 'oh I thought about it but...' and 'oh I wish I had done but...' Sometimes we don't listen enough to ourselves – we criticise ourselves. And I say 'just get on with it.'

She loves her work and, aside from a Friday night aerobics class, which is sacrosanct, finds it difficult to set aside specific 'home' time for herself. She admits things might have been different if she had children.

'I've always been very committed in the work that I do and give it 100% and more. I think that's me as a person – I'm like that in everything I do. So it does mean my work–life balance can sometimes go a bit funny.'

Always thinking ahead to new concepts, Penny doesn't rule out the idea of working for herself in the future.

'I'm interested in how to develop a Fairtrade model for developing countries', she says. 'At the moment the model is very much shaped so that you buy a commodity in developing countries and it's charged at a premium in developed countries. I'm very interested in changing that model in a different way, especially seeing how it can work for growers able to grow and sell the commodity in their own country and still make a decent living.'

Her passion for social enterprise is clear; she's intrigued by businesses that are commercially aware and produce profit, but are at the same time 'giving and delivering a different mechanism around social environmental aspects.'

She admits that marketing and business are in her blood.

'I started as a marketer and that will always be part of me. When I look back at my career I just didn't want to conform', she says contemplatively. 'I like to do things differently, because that's what marketing is. It's about experimenting. It's about one area of the business where you should be allowed to do things differently.'

With the growth in ethical shopping, more mainstream coffee companies are viewing Cafédirect as a competitor. Whilst many have introduced their own ethical products, Cafédirect maintains its pioneering stance in that 100% of its range is Fairtrade.

To further support its growth, Cafédirect went into partnership with Costa Coffee in 2000 to sell its Fairtrade coffee through the chain's numerous outlets. Additionally, through an initial partnership with the Compass Group, Cafédirect has cafés in 300 university sites in various formats, including a street-facing café on Regent Street, London, in partnership with the University of Westminster.

With Penny at the helm and to further boost expansion, Cafédirect then conducted what she describes as 'still the biggest and most successful ethical share issue', to raise funds for investment in new IT systems and marketing and, in particular, Teadirect and Cafédirect's foodservice market.

They launched in February 2004 and were fully subscribed within three and a half months, raising £5m. The issue attracted over four and a half thousand shareholders, the vast majority of which were small investors who wanted to buy into Cafédirect's vision and mission. 'We just didn't know if there would be people out there who would want to buy shares in Cafédirect and there were. I was really pleased', says Penny.

The move ensured that the ownership of the company now includes Cafédirect's customers, growers and staff. Indeed, growers own 4.9% of the company and sit on the board of directors. Says Penny; 'you've really got that connection so that the company and the brand are now owned by the growers and consumers. That for me is quite a personal achievement.'

Other achievements for Cafédirect include the accolades received for its products; their Organic Roast & Ground coffee was awarded 18.5/20 by the *Guardian*'s Ethical Shopper writer Dominic Murphy in October 2005 while Cocodirect Drinking Chocolate was voted best Fairtrade hot chocolate (*Observer Food Monthly*, February 2006). Cafédirect ranked the

Advice to other ENTREPRENEURS

Get on with it!

third most trusted brand in the UK in a *Reader's Digest* poll, (Marketing, April 2006) and won The National Social Enterprise Award in 2004.

Penny personally was voted 'Ethical Idol' by the UK's business community in 2006, and awarded the Dods and Scottish Widows Businesswoman of the Year. She was also shortlisted for a Morgan Stanley Great Britons Award in 2007.

Cafédirect now employs around 35 staff. Annual turnover was £21.6m in 2006 and pre-tax profits were £48,000. 'However', Penny is keen to emphasise, 'it was a year when we put more investment back into the company as well as increased our investment on these social programs for growers. And we paid around about £684,000, so if you actually added the £684,000 plus the £48,000 you can see the actual profit we made. But we decided to put a larger chunk of that profit towards helping the growers in building for their future.'

Penny is keen to move the company into new markets and see how Cafédirect can develop internationally:

> We've started, this year, to launch ourselves in Hong Kong and hope at the end of the year to launch in Singapore and Taiwan as well. We've also done a trial in Galeries Lafayette in Paris. Whilst that's exciting we have a market here in the UK that we need to build and to grow. We'd also like to extend who we trade with beyond the 37 groups that we currently work with across 12 countries.

In contemplating the success she's had in raising Cafédirect's profile and that of Fairtrade itself, Penny is unequivocal in her opinion: 'I think anyone who runs a business needs to know their business inside out. Whatever it is and whether it's women or men, if you run a business you need to know what makes it tick.'

IW

THE
CORE
BUSINESS PLC

May Jennings

If you want to get ahead, start early. And with the admission that her personal mantra is *'carpe diem* – seize the day', May Jennings is hot off the starting gun. Whilst currently The Core Business' brand director, at just 24, she was also the youngest director of a publicly listed company; all pretty heady stuff for someone just getting settled into her first full-time role.

May joined The Core Business in January 2005, one year after boss and industry stalwart, Stirling Murray, founded it. Stirling has worked in senior and international positions across brands including Estée Lauder, Revlon, Rimmel and, most recently, Bourjois. Together with seven other staff, May works out of the company offices in London's Primrose Hill.

The Core Business describes itself as a 'personal care and beauty management group that distributes beauty brands and assists companies and individuals in leveraging, diversifying and creating brands in the global beauty sector.' Or, as May puts it succinctly: 'our business is unique to our industry; nobody offers the breadth of expertise and experience we do. We make things happen.'

Clients have included Alliance Boots, Imedeen, Coco Ribbon and Sleek, and current clients include Realhair and Creatures. The Core Business also has the exclusive distribution rights of Elite Models Fashion beauty products in the UK.

May was brought on board after studying at the London College of Fashion and working part time at REN skincare and Smythson of Bond Street in bespoke stationary.

'It was never really fashion I wanted to go into, it was always cosmetics', she admits.

The course I did at the London College of Fashion was a BA Hons in Fashion Management and Marketing but if you think of cosmetics, they are fashion – everything is interconnected. At the time I didn't really want to work in clothing and I always knew from when I was about twelve that I wanted to go into some kind of cosmetics or toiletries thing. I did work experience in New York at MAC Cosmetics, I spent time at Jo Malone and was with her part time for two years and I worked at REN Skincare.

Currently engaged to be married to fiancé Louis, May relishes the balance ('at the moment!') she has between work and home life, saying 'I wouldn't say I was somebody who was a workaholic. I'm not really like that. I suppose I can do quite a lot in the day – and I don't feel like I need to be leaving the office at 11 o'clock at night.'

She met current boss, Stirling, when he guest lectured on marketing and promotion at the London College of Fashion.

He was giving a bursary to a marketing competition: whoever came up with the best development proposal for Bourjois would win. I headed a team that won the prize, and at the awards ceremony, he was standing at the buffet and I thought 'I need some work experience.' So I went up to him and asked for some and he gave me six weeks work. I had a great time at Bourjois but didn't really think we'd meet again, then I bumped into him at a restaurant in London and he said 'I've just set up my own business, give me a call when you graduate.'

She did and Stirling gave May her first full-time job six months later as a brand specialist. Within months, she was made a member of the Board and consequently became a director. 'It was great but a lot of hard work!' says May on her promotion.

May relishes her work with cosmetic brands

Being a director of an AIM (Alternative Investment Market) listed company is no easy task, I have to say. It's totally consuming because you are responsible in a totally different way to what you would normally be doing. You're very accountable. But it's varied and very creative, which I loved.

Stirling Murray had left Bourjois to start The Core Business, self-funding it from mid-2004.

'We were running as a consultancy as our main business at that time', explains May. 'To take the business further and build it up quickly, instead of going to the banks for more money, we decided to list on AIM. It was quite quick – I joined in January 2005 and we listed in March 2006.'

May says the listing makes the business both credible and accountable.

'If you're listed on AIM, there are obviously a huge amount of things you have to do. Cross the t's, dot the i's. It probably gives us respectability as a business, and makes us more heavyweight.' The Core Business expects to be profitable in 2008.

When it comes to assessing the competition, May and Stirling believe that The Core Business has something unique to offer.

I think our expertise is key because we can be working with Boots, for example, on commercial strategy, and we can be working with a very small client on a children's brand and we're able to do both those things. One is new product development and the other is commercial strategy. Then we also distribute brands on top of that.

Her favourite part of the job is developing a product from scratch 'and then seeing it in Harvey Nichols and Superdrug. That's probably the most fun part', she says, 'and all the stages in between; the getting involved with everything from copywriting right through to the design process and sourcing packaging.'

It makes little difference to May that the company wasn't her original baby. 'As a director I had a vested interest in the business to succeed', she says frankly.

She does, however, know her own strengths and what she has brought to the role: 'youth, dynamism and creativity. I'm not afraid of going the extra mile to talk to people and get in front of them', she says.

May has never felt her age to be an issue when dealing with clients.

'The funny situation', she says, 'is that I find that people think I am a lot older than I am so its not like people meet me and think immediately "she must be 20." Most people tend to think I'm in my late twenties. I remember once meeting a potential client and they obviously went online to look at our website and found out that I was 23 at the time. I think she started the meeting in a way that was more difficult because she said something like "I couldn't believe you were so young, is there a reason why it's on your website? It sort of put me off a bit!" She was very honest, but it's the only time that's ever happened.'

> ## Role MODEL
>
> I love reading about Estée Lauder and hope one day to have a mentor I can speak with regularly.

There has been one recent occasion, however, where May herself acknowledges her age proved a decisive factor. She stepped down as a director of the AIM listed company in July 2007 after 18 months, in advance of the completion of an acquisition deal which required each director of the PLC Board to take on warranties 'more than five times everyone's salary.'

The decision was based on her acknowledgement that at 24, she wasn't in a position to take on those kinds of liabilities. However, she continues to be a brand director of the company with all its associated responsibilities:

A lot of my daily work involves liaising with clients and suppliers and looking at clients, proposed designs, packaging and copy where I give my opinion on whether a brand is meeting its agreed objectives and if not, advise on how best to move forward. If I am working on a new project I meet with chemists, designers and packaging specialists to pull everything together and prepare critical paths to ensure everyone meets deadlines. When the project is well under way I meet with retailers to negotiate listings. I don't leave the office particularly late, and either head home to cook dinner for Louis or meet with friends for dinner – though when you enjoy your job you tend to be working even when you are shopping, as you are always looking at what retailers or your competitors are doing.

Coming from an entrepreneurial background (her family runs Jennings the bookmakers), May's one regret is not spending enough time talking to her father about his business before he died. She says her biggest champion is her mother.

She tries to spend as much time as possible with people she enjoys working with and, when asked about socialising with like-minded people, comments 'I don't know many people that are like-minded, but that is probably where you get the most inspiration – from those that don't think the same way as you do.'

Whilst she considers it an advantage being a woman in business, May firmly believes both men and women are essential to any successful venture; 'they are very different and look at everything in a unique way', she says.

She does not consider herself an inspirational figure, insisting she is 'just doing her job.' However, she was recently included in *Management Today*'s '35 women under 35' 2007 and it seems likely more accolades will follow.

May would love to eventually work for herself and is proud that she knew what she wanted to do so early on. Whilst she says she hasn't yet really 'made it', she's confident that everything is a 'work in progress'. But right now, there's one thing that's top of her agenda: 'my honeymoon!' she says.

Advice to other
ENTREPRENEURS

Follow your intuition, which I think women have an endless amount of.

Dame Mary Perkins

I **have a wardrobe of** glasses to go with different outfits and for different occasions. I particularly like the new brightly coloured plastic and metal frames that are around now', says Dame Mary Perkins, founder of Specsavers Opticians.

The 63-year-old mother of three and grandmother of seven set up the optical company in Guernsey with husband Doug in February 1984. They met on the first day of their optics degree at Cardiff University and, says Mary, 'we go back a long, long way. We were together very early on. We studied together, worked together and we couldn't imagine what it would be like if we were apart.'

Admitting that optometry runs in her blood (her father was also an optician), Mary has always harboured a desire to support independent young optometrists, especially women, who wish to own their own practices and need help in running their businesses.

On leaving university in 1966, she had a choice: either work for an optical company or start on her own. With Doug by her side, she chose the latter:

We'd never worked for anybody. It wasn't that easy back in those days because opticians weren't allowed to advertise so we just had an office each – it was up two flights of stairs over a bakery shop, next door to a doctor. You had to wait for people via recommendation really. It was a slow start. We're going back to 1965–66 so it was completely a national health business then. Now you have showrooms where you go in and choose frames but opticians weren't like that then. If you had a ground floor shop, you usually had blinds in the window and there were no window displays. You couldn't just walk in and try on frames; it was quite different.

They ran their chain (which grew to 23 stores) until 1980 then sold up, spending the following four years researching the market and waiting for deregulation from Margaret Thatcher's government to enable them to pursue their new venture.

Mary estimates that they invested around £500,000 into the fledgling Specsavers through the sale of those 23 stores, but admits she never kept tabs on the exact figure.

It wasn't some lump sum in the beginning but initially spending on advertising, being away from home, hotels…it all adds up. It wasn't an actual worry at the time, because we could always get a job and work as an optician. So it wasn't as though we were going to be on the streets!

They had a general idea of what they were doing but Mary admits that four years out of the business meant they were somewhat out of touch.

I did sort of know how to go about it but it was starting from scratch as we didn't have anything. You just go through all that process again; making contacts with new companies, buying equipment and the products, and employing staff. The only new thing for me was the advertising and the marketing because we'd never done that before – we weren't allowed to.

They had visited the USA to research the franchising of opticians.

'What I didn't want was a chain operation with a head office employing different opticians all over the country', explains Mary. 'I wanted opticians

Rose-tinted glasses: Mary always wanted to support young, independent optometrists

to own their own stores, which is what they do, but on a 50/50 basis. We would provide them with support services like marketing, accounting, IT etc., and leave them to get on with the day-to-day running of the business and to do what they do best, which is to test people's eyes and make sure they've got the right glasses and contact lenses for their needs. By providing them with back-up support it removes much of the strain of running a small company, allowing our opticians to offer the best possible service.'

Confident that they already knew their market well, Mary and Doug didn't feel a business plan was relevant for them:

> *I would strongly advise that everyone has one nowadays, but it was unnecessary for us at the time. We knew what we were doing; we certainly knew how to make the venture work but we had to get through that first year successfully so that we had some satisfactory figures to show other opticians so that they would join the group.*

They turned a profit within 12 months, a reflection of how well their unique vision and determination to remove the barriers for visits to opticians were being received by the public. Mary continues:

We were the first opticians to hire what I would call a showroom where people could walk in and try on frames. People used to come from miles just to look at it! This was all part of our vision to provide fashionable and affordable eyecare for everyone so that people could afford to have more than one pair, like opticians' wives did!

Mary explains how they encouraged optometrists to join the group:

At the time, opticians were seeing just a few people a week and charging high prices – they were making a good living. What we were saying was, lower the prices and you will see a lot more people and this will work much better. It will expand the market and people will visit the optician more often because glasses aren't so expensive. It was a slow process but we've had steady growth from year one. We've had continuous expansion ever since; even after the first year we were opening 20, 30 stores a year.

True to her word, the company today works in a joint venture partnership with local community optometrists, who own their businesses while Specsavers offers support services, including sourcing products, marketing, business development, finance, manufacturing and training.

'This means that we have more than 1,000 minds focused on moving the business forward all the time – you can't run retail from behind a desk in a head office', she says. 'We are strong on communication and the execution of projects. The marrying of professional eyecare with a high fashion service exceeds customer expectations on the retail side. We have 33% market share – three times that of our nearest competitor. Our initiatives are now being partly replicated by competitors but as the market is always changing, we can stay one step ahead of those who try to copy us.'

As the company has grown, Mary has been too busy to stop and wonder whether being a woman in business has been an advantage or disadvantage:

'Apart from two weeks, I didn't take time off to have my children and if I had to travel or stay away from home I did.' There was never an equal split between work and home life; 'not now and not when my children were small', she admits. 'In reality I work all hours and seven days a week.' She also admits to not seeing as much of her grandchildren as she'd like as she is kept so busy.

'We are still expanding globally', she says. 'Each country has its different challenges and this keeps us on our toes.'

Specsavers' expansion into the international market began with the Netherlands 10 years ago.

It was quite a big leap because, when you go to another country, even if you've got a winning formula and a winning business in the UK, it doesn't mean its going to translate anywhere else, even if you think it's going to. You really have to adapt to the needs of the local culture and the local people.

Specsavers now has 838 optical stores across Europe (604 in the UK and Ireland), 111 hearing centres (11 of which are overseas) and a supply chain to more than 150 stores in Australia.

As a privately owned company, Specsavers does not divulge its profits; however, turnover in 2006/7 was £879m with a staff of 15,000.

'There is no such thing as an average day in the life of Specsavers', says Mary cheerfully, although her day usually starts early with yoga ('with a teacher at my house – I would never do it on my own!'). She's extremely hands-on across most areas of the business, whether it's visiting stores, working on the shop floor, meeting opticians or visiting other Specsavers offices and laboratories.

In addition, I visit all countries we are in twice a year and now Australia, which is done in 20 day blocks. Each day is different. I've never not wanted to go to work. I have to say that everyone I work with are my friends, including all the joint venture partners in the Group – I meet them all at least four times a year.

Role MODEL

I particularly admire Baroness Susan Greenfield. She's really very good and I love listening to her speak because she doesn't stop! She's very good at telling you what makes people how they are and how they're changing and I find that quite interesting because optics has changed tremendously and so have the people who visit opticians. I wouldn't say she actually mentored me or acted as a role model but I do admire her as a person.

203

Even from the beginning, family values have been important to Mary; 'I've always felt that you spend an awful lot of time at work and it should be as pleasurable as possible. You've got to work hard but it should be enjoyable too.' To that end, Mary had spent the morning of our interview writing out birthday cards for staff. 'A few people have gone down with a virus, so I'm writing cards for them, too', she adds.

The emphasis on family values at work clearly starts from home – Mary's three children are all involved in the business. Her son is financial director and joint managing director, one daughter is country manager in the Netherlands and the other is in internal audit.

Comparing the experience of starting up a business now and in the 1980s, Mary is concerned at the red tape involved today:

Nowadays, there is an awful lot to do, even in small businesses; they've got so many things to look at such as health and safety regulations, disability compliance, employment law, etc. and I sometimes wonder if there are too many and too much paperwork for a small business. It never even crossed my mind when I started.

Mary was recently profiled as one of 10 top female entrepreneurs and was awarded for her entrepreneurial spirit in 2006. She says that she is most proud of receiving an Honorary Fellowship from her old college, Cardiff University, and becoming a Dame in the Queen's Birthday Honours List in 2007. 'A first in optics and a first in Guernsey!' she is quick to point out.

Specsavers as a business has also received many awards, most notably voted Britain's Most Trusted Brand of Optician by *Readers Digest* for the past six years running.

Advice to other ENTREPRENEURS

Involve the whole family so that they know why you are not always available to them.

Mary's success at Specsavers has enabled her to support her many charitable passions, including Age Concern, Women's Refuge, Vision Aid Overseas and Fight for Sight.

'Personally, I would like to expand my charity efforts, particularly with older people and organisations such as Action Aid, SightSavers and Diabetes UK – diabetes being the biggest cause of blindness in the UK.'

While Specsavers keeps an eye on what others in the industry are doing, Mary says they never set out to make money:

Obviously we wanted to run a profitable business for the sake of our partners and staff. I think the business has been so successful because we all passionately believe that we are offering the public what they want – a professional, caring service and quality, fashionable products at a price they can afford. Profits are ploughed back into the business to ensure that we continue to offer the best possible service, with up-to-date equipment and fresh-looking stores. We never rest on our laurels!

Romy Fraser

'**I suppose, looking back** on it', says Romy Fraser, 'it was quite hard, but I was really keen to make it work. I didn't really have any expectations; I didn't have a big, bold business plan. I didn't want to make it into anything particularly massive and it wasn't predetermined where it was going to go. I didn't have a huge amount to lose really, because I started with not a lot, so it was alright.'

The 60-year-old founder of Neal's Yard Remedies, famous for its organic and natural range of remedies as well as its trademark blue glass bottles, originally wanted to be a teacher. On completing her studies, she spent some time on a commune in Scotland before deciding to focus on her interest in homeopathy. She says there were two main elements that inspired her to launch her own business: she'd decided to set up her own school and had a keen interest in natural medicine:

I realised there was nowhere in mainland Europe that you could get homeopathic remedies and herbs and oils sold in one environment that people thought was knowledgeable and serious. Then the other strand was that I was a schoolteacher working in a really interesting school which had a particular style of teaching based on the belief that in order to help the child become a mature and fully able adult you needed to work with them and develop their own creative potential. It was all to do with empowerment really. We use that word too much, but that's what it was about.

A single mother, Romy never deliberately set out to found her business. In fact, she admits that 'business didn't really occur to me.' Instead, she was encouraged by her friend Nick Saunders, who owned the Neal's Yard Wholefoods business as well as some of its buildings.

He'd inspired a couple of other people to set up businesses – and funded them – and his idea was to make Neal's Yard into a sort of healthy, beautiful centre in London. He painted the buildings and put in window boxes, and I suggested to him that he should have an alternative pharmacy. A year or so later he got back to me and said he was selling the business, but his building, the retail part of his building, was then to be split into two and would I like to take half of that retail space? I think, frankly, he was looking for a good and sympathetic tenant.

Romy was upfront and confessed that she had neither the money nor the business experience and perhaps he should reconsider. Nick responded by guaranteeing her a loan of £18,000. It took her three years to pay it back.

Recalling that the shop was just an empty shell, Romy had to fit it out. 'My partner then painted it all to look the same – he was a paint specialist. He was brilliant and designed the logos as well. He was very instrumental in the business becoming a success.'

Romy never considered whether or not there was an actual market for her products; 'I didn't really think of it like that, I just thought, "well I like it, I think it's necessary, nobody else is doing it" and I just assumed that people would need it as much as I did.'

Launching in December 1981, Romy remained in the same shop for four years.

'It all happened quite slowly really', recalls Romy. 'To begin with it took me about nine months to set the business up and to work out what stock

Neal's Yard trademark blue glass bottles

was needed. We packaged everything ourselves, imported the bottles from France and designed the labels. There was quite a lot to do and we had to find out how to make a lot of the stuff. We got other people and contracted them to make it for us. It took some time for us to become well known and then people started asking us if we could supply them for their shops.

To begin with I was having to pack products in the back of the shop at night and it was getting really busy so I was pretty desperate for somewhere else to do it.'

Having made a profit by 1983 and in recognition of both public demand and the need for more space, Romy approached her bank manager for a loan and the local council for a development grant to finance a factory space in Battersea. They moved in 1985.

Romy estimates it took around nine months to turn 'this old builder's yard' in south London into a workplace. She admits it was difficult financially because she had created another cost centre.

I took over the old Neal's Yard Dairy shop in Chelsea farmer's market. Then I asked some of the people who were working in the company, 'do you want to do a remedies shop yourself?' and so a couple of people set up franchises. I drew up a franchise agreement, and a couple of people working in the shop went and set up their own shops. That instantly created two more shops so we had sales going out of four shops all together.

The first franchise was established in Oxford in 1986. Romy then took Neal's Yard Remedies to a trade show where she says 'we got ourselves established as a supplier of natural toiletries and the two sides of the company developed at the same time.'

By 1989 they were negotiating with stores in New York and Munich. The move to take Neal's Yard Remedies overseas was more to do with customer demand as opposed to a deliberate business decision. Romy says that it was the customers coming to them, by which time sales had reached over a million pounds.

Neal's Yard Remedies now turns over an estimated £9m a year and sells well over a thousand products across 24 countries. It currently has just under 30 stores around the UK and Northern Ireland and is stocked in John Lewis, Liberty and Waitrose. Most recently, the business was voted Best Ethical Brand 2007 by *The Sunday Times Style* magazine and Best Natural Range 2007 by *Natural Health* magazine.

Romy believes the selection of alternative medicines, essential oils and flower remedies she offered grew as a trend because of the way she ran the business.

We didn't wear white coats and set ourselves up as professionals, but we were actually all qualified or nearly qualified in one area of natural medicine or another. Everybody knew what they were talking about and the whole idea was to help people choose remedies for themselves. It wasn't us definitely saying 'ok, you've got this particular problem so you need to take this', it was engaging people in conversations about natural medicines, and giving them the options to choose from, which matched their symptoms. Of course we believe that everybody is an individual and everybody needs their own particular remedies rather than just saying 'ok, everybody with sleeping problems take this.'It wouldn't work as a general remedy for everyone.

In 2005, the company moved out of London and opened a new eco-friendly HQ in Dorset, specially designed by Feilden Clegg Bradley – architects well known for their environmentally sustainable buildings.

'Within our limits we have achieved a lot; certainly it's been designed to have a social heart', says Romy. 'You've got a meeting and café area in the middle of the factory where you can sit outside, and we've got organic food and subsidised natural health treatments so it's all quite nice. We didn't manage to get a crèche there but as it happens there's a good nursery next door. We planted an orchard and there's a vegetable garden where we grow our own vegetables. It's good.'

With her children helping out in the holidays, Romy doesn't make the usual distinctions between work and home life.

'They joined in with the business', she admits. 'Personal sacrifices are inevitable.

Role MODEL

I think there are several ethical and socially responsible businesses based in California that I was really impressed by during the 1980s. It was how they ran the businesses and had their ecological buildings, the paternity leave and just their approach to making the business an opportunity to communicate with other people and learn from other people. They were really inspiring. Seeing the staff canteen with organic food, how they encouraged people to cycle into work; they also included facilities for children as it is great having them in the workplace. It sort of humanises the workplace.

Everything in life's a balance isn't it? You choose to make a nice meal and you are sacrificing watching a film you wanted to see. You make choices which aren't easy choices to make. That's life. It would be odd if it wasn't like that.'

She's doubtful as to whether being a woman has had any real effect on her business life, believing instead it's more down to what you are like as a person.

'I've certainly had to work very hard and maybe that hasn't been great when you've also got to bring up two kids, but at the same time having a family means that you also have to stay balanced and they were very much the drive behind making it work', she says.

In fact, she wasn't daunted in setting up a company and raising her children at the same time. 'You do', she says frankly, 'what you have to do.'

At the end of 2005, recognising that she was more interested in the quality of the products than securing further market share, Romy took a back seat as Peter Kindersley, organic farmer and founder of publisher Dorling Kindersley, bought a controlling stake in the company for an estimated £10m.

Advice to other ENTREPRENEURS

It's hard not to be clichéd, but I think when you are choosing what you do, choose something you're going to enjoy doing. Otherwise what's the point in doing it just for money? Make other people's lives richer. Do it to enjoy achieving what you want to achieve. Set up a business because you really want to do that business. When you're doing it, create a working environment that you'd want to work in. Make it enjoyable for the people that work with you.

I suppose, in a way, it was not so much the competition but the need to sell more and more and more. That didn't really interest me. If you can constantly improve what you're doing and how you're doing it, then it carries on being an interesting challenge. I think if you focus on just grabbing more of the market it's pretty boring.

Romy still keeps herself involved in the business, focusing on specific PR projects and product development. 'I do bits and pieces', she says.

Romy thinks men can be just as ethical as women can when it comes to founding their businesses. Instead, she believes it's more about what motivates you to drive the business. For her, it was a determination to introduce natural remedies to the public rather than money.

> *As long as I earned enough to support myself and my family then that was OK. I was just interested in making it work in order to enable more people to have access to natural medicines, and that's why I set up more shops, set up courses, and did staff training. I was very keen to do things with the best quality possible, which meant that it had to be organic and I had to keep the packaging to a minimum and to recycle it. Doing things ecologically means you're doing things sensibly, because if you recycle, it actually makes financial sense as well. I don't waste anything and I was very careful with how I spent the money and how we used time. If you do all of those things you naturally become what is now called an ethical business. I don't think being a woman really has a huge amount to do with it. Maybe it's possible that I was more interested in the social side of the business and building that side of it than most men would.*

In looking back over what she's achieved, Romy says her journey has been well worth it. 'I've met so many amazing people, so many. I've learnt so much. It's been incredible.'

Alison Chow and Sophie Oliver

'**P**ants and thongs are big business. We've literally sold thousands in the past six months', says Alison Chow, co-founder of luxury lifestyle brand, Coco Ribbon.

The 35-year old Australian met business partner, 35-year old Sophie whilst they were working together in luxury brand fashion PR. The idea for Coco Ribbon, a London-based emporium stocking everything from luxurious lingerie to antique French furniture, evolved from working alongside many brands on a PR level. Alison and Sophie spotted a gap in the market for a young and quirky brand created especially to indulge and inspire women of all ages.

'We both knew we wanted to do something we love.' says Alison. 'When you work so hard in a job for someone else you wonder why you're doing it for someone else when you could be putting that energy into something that's your own.'

Founding Coco Ribbon was a natural progression on both their career paths rather than a hankering from an early age. 'One thing just led to another', says Sophie.

Opening its Notting Hill Gate doors to the public in 2002, Coco Ribbon has swiftly become the must-visit location for women who relish a boudoir shopping experience.

'It's for women of all ages, from five-year-olds wanting butterfly clips to 60-year-old women who come in and buy soap for Mother's Day', says Alison of the store, styled as a luxurious walk-in living room. 'But the thing they have in common is that they are women who look after themselves or like treating other people.'

Alison has been in the UK for eight years, following a two-year stint in Hong Kong. 'I've been away for quite a while', she laughs. 'I go home at least once or twice a year.'

'She hasn't lost her accent!' says Sophie.

'When we first made the decision to do what we wanted to do, it snowballed very quickly', says Sophie. 'We just wanted to do something that we loved and the name comes from our two favourite things – chocolates and ribbons. We decided the shop was going to be full of those favourite things so we just put the two names together.'

Their initial funding came through investing savings and money raised by Alison remortgaging her house, a total of £37,500 each.

They prepared a detailed business plan which took them around 12 months to 'fine tune' and approached the Portobello Business Centre ('who were amazing') for business support and advice; the plan eventually won an award from the Centre, giving Alison and Sophie the impetus to 'give it a go', says Sophie.

As for the shop's location, Sophie says it was 'pretty much the first or the second place that we found. I just think it was complete karma. It's a lovely store which has a lovely feeling about it; it was definitely meant to be. It took us quite a while to secure it.'

'We were lucky', says Alison, 'and the person who was here before us was here for 10 years which is always a good sign. You never want to move into a property that keeps turning over and turning over.'

They agree that their biggest challenge in setting up was the logistics of getting everything ready to open on time, from store design and stock to staff and organising the back office.

Coco Ribbon offers the ultimate luxurious shopping experience

Coco Ribbon tripled what they forecast for their first year turnover and became profitable in its first quarter. Says Sophie:

We've been very lucky. From the beginning we've had some brilliantly loyal staff, not just on the sales side but on the back office side. It's all about communication and training and making sure that everyone knows what's going on; making them part of the company. I think also that Alison and I, having worked for a long time for other people, know how we want to be treated in a work environment. We want the girls to enjoy coming into work and our business.

'And be part of the bigger picture', adds Alison.

That's important because a lot of the girls we employ are educated, so they're smart, they're all-rounders with great personalities. Working for other people, you never get to use all your creativity and ability and sometimes that can be frustrating. But when you have a boss that says 'hey, if you come up with any great ideas for marketing or for VIPs, then we'd love to hear that' you give them that opportunity and that keeps them happier and around for longer.

Sophie and Alison have now worked together for eight years. 'We're quite different and it works really well', says Sophie, who describes herself as very much a 'back office' woman, admitting that whilst very messy at home, at work she's meticulous. 'I do spreadsheeting. I like my lists and try to keep on top of budgets and financials', she says.

Sophie describes Alison as 'very creative, full of ideas and great at networking.' She pushes the business from an outwards perspective.

'We always do things differently. We don't stand still, we are constantly evolving and we try to do things in a way which is new and innovative', says Alison.

Their must-have goodies are sourced from all over the world and the store has become a respected platform for talented new designers, especially from Alison's hometown of Sydney, Australia.

'Working with suppliers there is always a delicate balance between who needs who more', says Alison.

In a way we're quite lucky because a lot of people do want to be stocked with us and from that they're a little bit more flexible. We have a good relationship and good communication with them but at the same time you have to be assertive and get better terms and discounts. It is a business. At the beginning it's hard if you're friendly with these people but you've got to know when to be assertive and I think anyone in business respects that. We've got a lot of suppliers that we've kept for the last five years, which is quite good considering we change our product range quite a lot.

The majority of the purchasing decisions are left to their 'brilliant and fashion forward' buyer, although when they first started, it was more about what they both liked.

'You have to stand back and look at what you've created', says Sophie of the experience of working for herself. 'For me, I come into work and I don't even think about it. But getting someone else's perspective on what we do, someone who says "I love your shop, I love what you do", it's only then you step back and think "oh my God!"'

'When I used to work for other people I'd dread coming into work', continues Alison.

I'd get Sunday-itis, Monday-itis. That dread of getting up early and going into work. I didn't like working for other people at all – it was so regimented. Even though I work harder now than in our previous jobs, I never dread coming into work at all. You're doing your thing and you're the master of your own destiny. You decide what you're doing during the day – there's no one telling you how, what to do or when to do it.

Coco Ribbon has won numerous awards, including Time Out Best Independent Retailer 2004, Time Out Top 100 shops 2005 and Coolbrands 2006/07. Alison and Sophie were also nominated for a business award in 2006.

Whilst Alison says its 'great to have the acknowledgement' of those awards and achievements, for Sophie, their proudest moment is getting to where they are today, 'where we are about to embark upon our next project – our own line of clothing, accessories and cosmetics. It is an amazing feeling.'

They admit with hindsight they would have done certain things differently but see everything they do as part of a growth process. Warns Sophie:

The financial environment for two women in business can be quite difficult. You do come across certain types of people where it's a battle to be taken seriously. For two women – especially two women who have opened a boutique – even though we have moved on from that to do our own line, it's sometimes a bit of a cliché that some people find quite predictable.

Alison says that dealing with the banks has been a huge challenge because 'they don't understand entrepreneurs a lot of the time. It's hard to explain what we're trying to achieve with our brand to middle-aged men who don't get it.'

Role **MODEL**

Jo Malone & Anya Hindmarch.

Advice to other
ENTREPRENEURS

Planning and believing in yourself
that it can be done!

'There are a lot of guys who 'get' the store and how it works', says Sophie, 'but it's very difficult for certain men to fathom exactly what it is that we do. Therefore they don't take us seriously. We've spent a long time proving ourselves in that area.'

Alison agrees with Sophie's admittance that 'work tends to overpower family life at the moment', but both try to and split it as equally as they can.

'It's all about being fantastically organised!' says Sophie. 'Being a mother and businesswoman is one of the most difficult things I have tackled.'

Sophie adds that her biggest sacrifice in building up Coco Ribbon has been quality time with her husband and friends, whilst for Alison, it's more a question of homesickness.

'I'm doing this for my family and myself', says Sophie. 'When we started five years ago, I was living with my partner but leading a very different life and ultimately the business was for me. Now, my priority is my family. I am ultimately doing this because I love it and because it will make a difference to us in the long-term.' Alison agrees: 'I'm doing it for me now and for my future.'

After their experiences in setting up Coco Ribbon, they are both adamant that returning to work for someone else would be difficult, and unlikely.

The next step is to take their boudoir boutique concept global. 'We're working on our own fashion line and our own line in lots of different avenues. We'd love to be stocked internationally', says Sophie. 'We're working on it and we're going to have agents pushing us forward in different countries. Ultimately, it would be lovely to have Coco Ribbon stores in places overseas. We really have our eyes set on the international market.'

'We try to split our roles so that they don't cross and so that we can cover most things as efficiently as possible. We've got quite a few different elements; the website, product development, gifts and accessories and then there's the store, so there's a lot to do', says Alison.

They both love seeing the Coco Ribbon label on their goods. 'It makes us realise how much we have achieved', says Sophie.

'I don't know many people who go out and say "I want to be an entrepreneur"', says Alison finally. 'You've either got that spirit in you or you don't. If you know how you like things and you're frustrated that you can't find them – or you think you've seen a gap in the market or ways to do things better – then it's just a natural drive.'

———— *IW* ————

Other inspiring business success stories:

HOW THEY STARTED

How 30 Good Ideas Became Great Businesses

This book is about 30 ordinary people who had an idea and went on to turn it into a hugely successful business.

From direct interviews with the founders of each company this features many house-hold names such as Dyson, Cobra Beer, innocent drinks, Pizza Express and Gu Puds. This books shows how these people started from scratch and answers many questions about how they got off the ground, including: how much did it cost, how thy chose the name, how they sourced suppliers, and how they got their fi rst customers.

I certainly wish we'd had this book when we were starting innocent.
Richard Reed, joint founder, innocent Drinks

Although in business there is no substitute for making the leap and getting started, there is much to be learned from entrepreneurs who have been there and done it. Live the highs and lows for yourself, but read this book first.
Lord Bilimoria, founder & chief executive

Author: David Lester
Published: June 2007
ISBN: 978-1-85458-400-7

MALE ORDER

The Charles Tyrwhitt Story

An inspiring and dramatic account of the founding of Charles Tyrwhitt Shirts, one of the most successful mail-order companies in Britain today, with a turnover of £50 million. The story of an entrepreneurial journey, told through anecdotes, by founder Nicholas Wheeler himself.

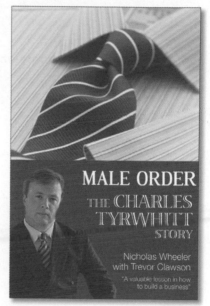

Wheeler gives an honest account of the highs and lows of running his business. From the initial start-up and growth, the crisis when he lost the business and his brave determination and effort in order to buy the company back again, to his involvement in the business today,

Author: Nicholas Wheeler with Trevor Clawson
Published: February 2008
ISBN: 978-1-85458-403-8

www.crimsonpublishing.co.uk